The Complete Book of Midwifery

The Complete Book of
Midwifery

✤ ✤ ✤

Barbara Brennan, C.N.M., and Joan Rattner Heilman

E. P. DUTTON & CO., INC. | NEW YORK

List of nurse-midwifery services courtesy Legislation Committee of the American College of Nurse-Midwives and is excerpted from their publication "Legislation and Nurse-Midwifery Practice in the USA," *Journal of Nurse-Midwifery*, Vol. XXI, No. 2, Summer, 1976.

Photos by Suzanne Szasz appear courtesy of Good Housekeeping.

LIBRARY OF CONGRESS CATALOGING IN PUBLICATION DATA

Brennan, Barbara.
    The complete book of midwifery.

    Includes index.
    1. Midwives—United States. 2. Maternal health
services—United States   I. Heilman, Joan Rattner,
joint author. II. Title.
RG960.B73 1977   618.4   76-29359
ISBN: 0-525-03180-4

Published simultaneously in Canada by Clarke, Irwin & Company Limited, Toronto and Vancouver

To my family and especially to my Aunt Marger

Contents

Introduction

Ever since we started the first midwifery service for private patients at Roosevelt Hospital in New York City in 1974, I have been doing a lot of talking. Suddenly, everyone—potential patients, television studios, newspapers, magazines, other hospitals—wants to know about certified nurse-midwives, our function, our methods, our philosophy, as well as just how our new program works.

Midwifery-managed pregnancies and deliveries have become, almost overnight, a real alternative to the usual birth experience for women who are in a position to choose the kind of care they want. We are no longer serving only to relieve the doctors of an overwhelming load of clinic deliveries; rather, we offer a unique option for women who want to have an increased participation in the birth of their children.

Our program has attracted women from all sectors of the population. They have included teachers, lawyers, students, housewives, doctors, doctors' wives, and nurses. At a time when many hospitals are considering closing their obstetric departments because of the declining birth rate, our hospital has found a marked increase in its deliveries. Grounded in history, certified nurse-midwifery is a truly contemporary phenomenon, one that is gaining widespread acceptance.

I am writing this book because I want to tell every woman who is having a baby, or thinking about having a baby, just who and what certified nurse-midwives are and what we can offer her. This will also be the account of a personal journey; I have been privileged to see the renascence of midwifery in the U.S. and to play an active part in it.

I want to get across to expectant mothers and fathers the message that childbirth can be a joyful experience—hard work, but immensely rewarding. I want to tell them that they are the ones who are having their babies, not the medical experts, and so they can have them the way they want to. I want them to have a positive feeling toward their pregnancies, a respect for their bodies' connection with their babies. I want them to know it is possible to have a truly personalized childbirth.

There has been increasing dissatisfaction for years with the kind of care women have traditionally received in childbirth. Pregnant women have often been treated as if they have a disease that must be ruthlessly cured. They have been patronized and routinized, knocked out by drugs, separated first from their husbands, then from their babies because of rigid hospital rules. They have been made to feel they have nothing to do with their own child's birth except to give the medical experts as little trouble as possible and to pay huge fees. They have been put through unpleasant procedures because these procedures are part of the regular agenda—whether they need them or not—and sometimes given medical treatment that may have been seriously harmful to their babies. They have been left alone to labor in fear and pain, and they have had little emotional support at the time they need it most. At the very least, they have come to feel like an unimportant cog in a huge machine.

That is why, when women found out about nurse-midwives, there was such intense interest in us.

Professional midwives look at pregnancy and childbirth as a normal process, something a woman's body is designed to do and can do by itself 9 times out of 10—by giving the woman little more than reassurance, encouragement, guidance, and a pair of helping hands. We specialize in normal pregnancies and normal, spontaneous deliveries and provide total maternity care as part of a team practicing in hospitals or maternity homes with obstetricians who serve as emergency back-up in case of complications.

This book is not written to criticize the doctors nor to suggest we replace them. I have known, and know, many marvelous obstetricians who give their patients exactly the kind of care we do. But we all know many who do not, partly because as men (the vast majority of doctors are male) they cannot possibly understand a woman as well as another woman can; partly because they have had years of training in dealing with emergencies and find it hard to let nature work its own miracles without interference; and partly because they are overworked and truly busy. I feel that the doctors can best address themselves to the complicated cases—the abnormal—while we address ourselves to the normal pregnancies and pay attention to the demands women are making.

Change is in the air. The midwife, who used to be the "granny," an untrained birthing assistant, is now the certified nurse-midwife who is a specialist (with obstetric nursing experience and graduate training in midwifery). But she has the attitudes and the approach of the age-old profession, and that is what women today are seeking.

They are seeking a different kind of care, and they are seeking a voice in their own destinies. It is because of this

tremendous new interest in childbirth—and so midwives—
that I am writing this book.

Acknowledgment must go to all those who have done so
much for our profession in general and, in particular, our
enterprise at Roosevelt Hospital: Midwives Eldra Simmons,
Jeanne Kobritz, Mary Dowd, Dorinda Dew, Nancy Cud-
dihy, and Sandra Woods, who have worked so closely with
me in bringing about this new concept; the hospital's obstetricians, who have backed us up in all ways every minute
of every day, especially Dr. John Dwyer; the nursing staff,
whose professional contributions are constant and excellent;
the nurse-anesthetists, who stand by for each delivery; and
the pediatricians, who have given such good care to our
newborns. And to Dr. Thomas Dillon, director of obstetrics
and gynecology at Roosevelt Hospital, who had the vision
and made it happen.

1

One Woman's Story

"The difference between the birth of this baby and the birth of our other daughter eight years ago is overwhelming. It is absolute and complete. Nothing was the same—nothing.

"I had my first baby in a mid-Southern city. She was delivered by the most respected obstetrician in town and in one of the top hospitals. The doctor was a charming man, and naive as I was then, I was delighted when he said, 'We'll take care of everything. Don't you worry.' He was a real Big Daddy, the kind of man who would literally pat me on the shoulder when I seemed concerned about anything.

"I remember asking him about natural childbirth, and he said, 'When you come to the hospital, and you feel like natural childbirth, you can have it.' I thought, That's really great. Looking back, I can't believe I was so ignorant as well as trusting.

"When I finally went into labor and got to the hospital, the doctor wasn't there. He had said to me on the telephone when I called to tell him my contractions were close and getting strong, 'You go on in. Call me if you need me, but you're not going to have the baby for a long time, maybe not till sometime tomorrow.' Later I found out he was going to his daughter's Sweet Sixteen party.

"So, there I was, shaved and enemaed, in the labor room with my husband. We were there alone except for periodic visits from the nurse and occasionally a resident. As the contractions grew stronger and more painful, I screamed for the nurse, who went out and came back with an injection for me—orders, evidently, of the doctor. Almost immediately I fell asleep, only to be wakened in terror by a huge contraction. When it was over, I fell asleep again until the next one jolted me into panicked consciousness. That's the way it went, for hours.

"My husband, left alone with this screaming, writhing, tormented woman, was totally unsettled, and after a few hours, when the nurse said, 'It will be a while, why don't you go home?' he was relieved to go.

"What I remember of that drugged labor was one long continuous pain. I had no control over my mind or my body. I was simply in the grip of the kind of torture I didn't think I could bear any longer.

"Finally, the doctor came, though I don't remember it, and the baby was delivered. If I saw her in the delivery room, I don't recall it. When I woke up in a haze in the recovery room, I could barely remember why I was there. I felt no connection with the baby and no interest in her at all. Even when I was back in my room, and they brought her to me, it was as if she wasn't mine. It took me a long time—months—to develop my love for her.

"I never blamed the doctor for anything. I thought that was the way it had to be. But the older and wiser I got, and the more I talked to other women about their childbirth experiences, the more I realized that he had really betrayed me. He knew what was going to happen and how I'd respond to the pain. Why hadn't he told me, why hadn't someone told me, what to expect?

"It took a long time for us to decide to have another baby, and when I was pregnant, my husband said to me, 'I can't believe you'd want to go through that again. What about a cesarean?' He asked that again and again throughout the pregnancy.

"I had already made an appointment with an obstetrician when I heard, from a friend, about the midwives at this hospital. I spoke to Barbara on the phone and asked her a hundred questions. By this time I'd become very smart about childbirth; I'd read everything, talked to everyone. I knew I wanted to be right there this time, awake and in control of things. I didn't want any drugs; I wanted George there; I wanted to nurse the baby on the delivery table; I wanted to learn how to cope with the contractions and have this baby myself. There were loads of things I wanted—and I could have them all, according to Barbara, if everything went normally.

"I think the single most important feature that sold me was the promise that a midwife would stay with us in the labor room. Even if you took forever, she'd be there. The idea was unbelievably comforting to both of us.

"From my very first prenatal visit, the experience was completely different from the last time. Maybe it was because I was raised to think that doctors were gods, but I've always been embarrassed to ask male doctors intimate questions or to take up too much of their time. I was afraid to demand too much attention. But right at the beginning the midwife asked me more questions about myself and my family's health history than I'd ever been asked before; she examined me and explained who the midwives were, what they were here for, what they did, and what their boundaries were. Then she sat back and asked if I had any questions. I had a lot, and I asked them all, and I never got the feeling I was asking a stupid question. I got answers to everything, and she never stood up or looked at her watch once.

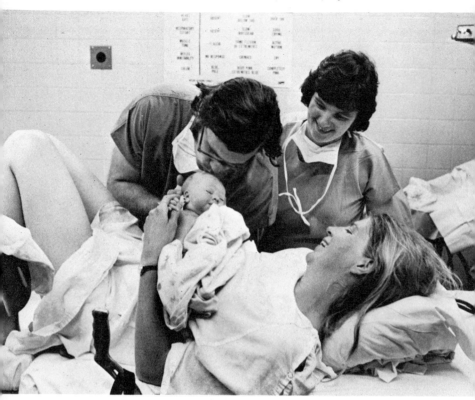

Photo by Suzanne Szasz

"That's the way it was in all the visits to Roosevelt, each time with a different one of the five midwives. I never felt uptight or embarrassed about any of my normal woman's functions or feelings. Maybe it was because they were women, too, or maybe because I knew they weren't bored with my uneventful progress.

"This time, George and I went to the prepared-childbirth classes, where we made it our business to learn everything we could about what was going to happen. I think he would still have preferred a cesarean, though. Our first pregnancy had obviously had a devastating effect on him.

"We went into the hospital one afternoon in March. The contractions were already good and regular, and the midwife told us I was already two centimeters dilated. No shave, no enema, no intravenous tube, but I was hooked up to the fetal monitor for part of the time to be sure the heartbeat was strong. No drugs except for a tiny amount toward the end to get me through the worst of it.

"George helped me with my breathing and massaged my back, with the midwife relieving him part of the time. Between contractions we talked about everything from babies to politics—until the end, when I wanted no distractions from my concentration. Just as they'd promised, the midwife never left us. I'll be eternally grateful for that because you want someone there who *knows*. George was terrific, but he was uncertain, too, and wouldn't have been at all happy left in charge of me. This way, there was no panic— it was like having a doctor there who is also your mother and your friend.

"I was so in control of my breathing and my contractions that when she told George he'd better go change into his delivery-room outfit, he was surprised—how could the baby be coming when I obviously hadn't suffered very much?

"The delivery was fast, very quiet and calm. In the mirror we watched the baby come out and touched her as she lay on my stomach before the cord was cut. They cleaned her up and gave her to me to feed. It was all happy feelings, and everyone in the room seemed to be as thrilled as we were. It was as though we'd all accomplished something together.

"Now I'm going to tell you something that sounds so corny, but it's true, and it's magnificent. I'd had another daughter for eight years, and I wondered if I could ever love another child as much, and if it would take me very long to learn to love it. But the minute the baby popped out, I was overwhelmed with love for her. It filled me up, that love, so much that I'll never forget that feeling. I could tell by his voice and the look on his face that George was feeling the same way.

"By the time we went home—the three of us—a day and a half later, it was as if we knew her well. She was part of us already.

"I have two children now, and I don't expect ever to have another child, but if I do, it will be partly because I want to go through that experience again."

2

Who Am I?

My Great-aunt Kate was a midwife. With her competent hands and comforting words, she delivered half the babies in South Amboy, New Jersey, around the turn of the century—including my mother. Aunt Kate was self-taught. She learned "birthing" on the job, apprenticing to an older, more experienced woman till she could take over on her own, letting nature take its course and helping it along as best she could. She was a lay midwife, the old-fashioned kind you can still find in some rural pockets of the land.

I, too, am a midwife but a thoroughly modern counterpart of Great-aunt Kate. I am a professional midwife, a C.N.M. (Certified Nurse-Midwife), which means I have completed an intensive midwifery education program with a strong emphasis on family and public health. To go on to become a midwife, I first had to be a registered nurse, with additional job experience as an obstetric nurse. I am a highly trained specialist.

There are over 1,800 certified nurse-midwives in the U.S. today, according to Dorothea M. Lang, C.N.M., current

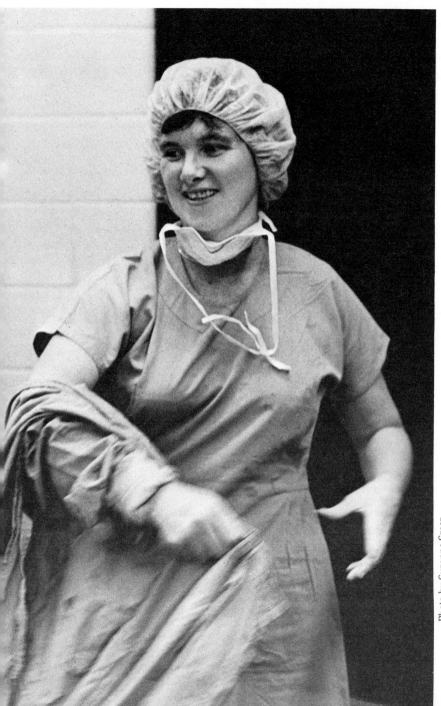

Photo by Suzanne Szasz

president of our professional organization, the American College of Nurse-Midwives (ACNM), and the director of the New York City Health Department's Nurse-Midwifery Service Program, whose midwives deliver about 3,500 babies a year. Approximately 1,000 midwives are members of the ACNM, and perhaps two-thirds of these are practicing their profession—that is, managing pregnancies, providing health care for women, and delivering babies. Each year, an additional 150 or more nurse-midwives graduate from the midwifery programs. Most of us work in large urban centers—there are about 100 in New York City alone—though some carry on our traditional role of bringing care to the rural poor.

Right now, all but three states in the nation permit nurse-midwives to practice. (Michigan, Wisconsin, and Massachusetts are the exceptions, although in at least one of these states—Massachusetts—legislation that could change this is pending.) There are some 150 separate midwifery services now in the country, with more being organized each month. These include services in hospitals, in city and state health departments, and in military bases, as well as maternity homes and obstetrician/midwife teams in private practice.

Though I was among the very first nurse-midwives to be educated in the U.S. (and that was only 14 years ago!), I've never thought of myself as a pioneer. And though I have helped bring about some rather radical changes in the way childbirth is conducted, I didn't become a midwife in order to make waves in the traditional order of things. My goal was to do a good job, doing what I loved to do.

I'm a midwife because I get a tremendous thrill out of delivering babies. To bring a new human being into the world calmly, peacefully, and happily gives me a marvelous feeling of excitement and accomplishment—even after all these years and more than 2,000 deliveries. I am not a doctor, though I have many of the same duties. I'm not an as-

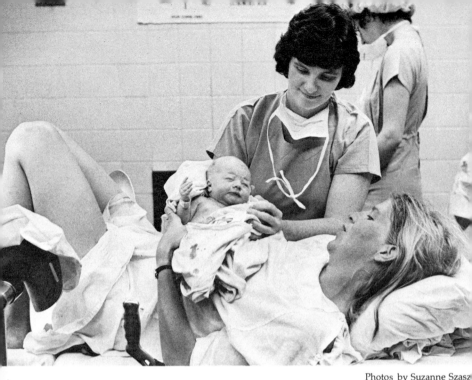

Photos by Suzanne Szasz

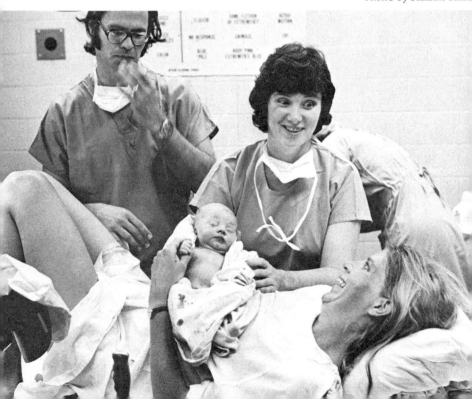

sistant doctor or an obstetric assistant. Nor am I a nurse anymore. I am a midwife, specifically trained to help normal, healthy women deliver normal, healthy babies.

Today's modern midwives specialize in *only* normal pregnancies, normal labor, and normal, spontaneous deliveries with little or no intervention. We are not trained to treat sick people or to handle complicated abnormal pregnancies. That's the job of a doctor. It is for this reason that midwives are never independent practitioners but are always members of an obstetric team, with the 24-hour-a-day "back-up" of physicians, who will work with us if their medical skills are needed.

Pregnancy is not a disease. It's not an injury or an assault on the body. It is a very natural and normal physiologic event about 90 percent of the time. Except in a small number of cases, all that is really needed from the outside world is reassurance, advice, and an extra pair of helping hands. The woman and her baby do most of the work themselves. Labor is just that—labor, hard work—and birth is the end result. We are there to *assist* in the process, not to *do* it.

> *"I felt like she really cared about me, like she was my friend-mother. You know this could be her 7,000th baby, but you get the feeling this baby counts."*

Normal, natural, uncomplicated pregnancies are definitely *not* boring to us, as they seem to be to many physicians who have spent years and years learning how to handle emergencies and perform major surgery. Our excitement comes not from performing intricate cesarean sections or from deftly wielding a pair of forceps but from helping a woman do a job her body was beautifully designed to do. You can't imagine the exhilaration I feel when one of my patients, who has been wide awake and working hard in

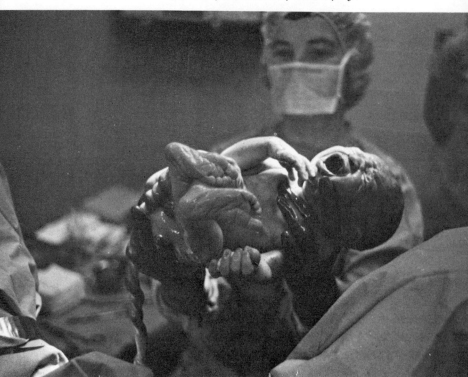

Photo by Gary Young

partnership with me, delivers a bright, alert, healthy baby into my assisting hands. We both know then that we, two women going about women's business, have taken part in a miracle.

The word "midwife" (which literally means "with the woman" in Old English) was not a respectable word in this country until just a few years ago. It conjured up images of old women with dirty hands and stained clothes, delivering babies in hovels while burning herbs at the foot of the bed.

But midwives have once again become respected in the U.S., as they always have been in other highly developed countries (such as England, the Netherlands, France, Nor-

way, Sweden, and Denmark). Because we are well educated, intensively trained in certified schools affiliated with
renowned universities and medical centers, and because we
have, in a few short years, earned a reputation for giving
women what they want in childbirth—dignified, sympathetic, safe, individualized, natural, nonroutinized care—
we are now in great demand. In fact, the demand is so great
that training programs can't educate us fast enough, and
there are long waiting lists for every midwifery school. For
each nurse-midwife trained in this country today, there are
at least ten jobs waiting for her or *him.* (There are three male
C.N.M.s at this writing.)

We have been discovered by the middle-class woman, the
woman who could and would pay for the services of the
best obstetrician in town if that's what she wanted. When
Roosevelt Hospital became the first voluntary hospital in
the country to offer midwifery care to private patients, we
were—and still are—swamped with applicants, to the point
where we've had to turn away hundreds of women because
we can't accommodate them.

>   *"I always used to think midwives were for people who
>   couldn't afford the real thing."*

What exactly is a certified nurse-midwife? Here is the def-
inition given by the ACNM: "The nurse-midwife is a registered nurse who, by virtue of added knowledge and skill
gained through an organized program of study and clinical
experience recognized by the ACNM, has extended the
limits of her practice into the area of management of care of
mothers and babies throughout the maternity cycle so long
as progress meets criteria accepted as normal."

What all this means is that certified nurse-midwives are
experts in managing normal pregnancies and delivering
babies when there are no medical abnormalities. We are
also trained in family planning, which means methods of

birth control, and can advise and help women between pregnancies not to conceive until they want to. We give gynecologic examinations. We help new mothers learn to care for their babies, including how to breast-feed. Many midwives are on the faculties of respected medical and nursing schools, teaching students normal obstetrics. Others specialize in conducting prepared-childbirth classes.

The number of C.N.M.s who manage and deliver *private* paying patients today is exceedingly limited. There are only a few hospitals and private obstetrician/midwife teams existing in the country that provide private deliveries, though the number is now growing steadily because of the new and overwhelming demand for them. Most midwives work where their expertise is most needed, with clinic populations, or combine clinic with a few private patients.

"My doctor came to the hospital right after I did. He examined me, and then I never saw him again until the delivery 14 hours later."

Right now, most women who wish midwife deliveries must become clinic patients, and many women who could afford private care are doing just that. At Downstate Medical Center at Kings County Hospital in Brooklyn, N.Y., for example, the midwives report that a high percentage of their patients now come to the clinic because they want midwifery care. And in a rough ghetto neighborhood, also in Brooklyn, women from outside the community with the means to go elsewhere have been finding their way to the midwives.

When Roosevelt Hospital recruited me 13 years ago to become the first nurse-midwife employed by a voluntary hospital, there was no thought that I would work with private patients. And for 10 years I didn't. I, and the four midwives who were subsequently hired, cared solely for clinic patients. But, in 1974, when we began our private service for women on the higher socioeconomic scale, the professional midwife became truly accepted as a valid alternative to the usual childbirth experience. Now women are beginning to have a choice between physicians and midwives, and other hospitals that have been watching our "experiment" closely have begun to follow our example.

> *"I have no complaints about the obstetrician who delivered my first two babies. He was marvelous, and I just loved him. But we moved East, and we couldn't use him this time. When I started looking for another doctor, a friend told me about the midwifery service, and it sounded perfect for me. It has turned out that way, too. I couldn't have asked for a happier experience."*

To become a certified midwife, one must attend a nationally approved educational program in midwifery. There are now 15 schools offering midwifery programs, all of them affiliated with well-known schools of nursing, medicine, allied health, and/or public health. By 1977, when this book is published, all must have a university affiliation. (The schools presently offering midwifery programs include Yale University, the University of Illinois, Frontier School of Midwifery and Family Nursing in Kentucky, University of Kentucky, Johns Hopkins University, United States Air Force, University of Mississippi, St. Louis University, State University of New York, Columbia University, Meharry Medical College, University of Utah, University of South Carolina, New Jersey Medical College, and Georgetown University.)

Two routes may be taken by students: (1) The basic midwifery course, which results in a certificate, varies in length from 9 to 12 months; (2) Those of us who have bachelor's degrees may choose to earn a certificate along with a master's degree, which takes one to two years of training. And some of us have gone on to get Ph.D. degrees.

Several midwifery schools and services provide internships, which are for recent graduates who wish to have more supervised clinical experience before taking a job. And in addition to these programs there are also refresher courses given in many institutions. Professionals who have been educated in midwifery in other countries, and who must be introduced into the American system, comprise most of this group, though there are also those midwives who have not practiced their profession for more than five years, and who must receive this additional training before resuming their practice.

> *"When my friend told me about the program here, I couldn't believe it. I'd never even heard of midwives except from the history books. But when I found out that they were real professionals with all kinds of training and experience, I decided to come here. What a difference this delivery has been!"*

By the time we have finished our specialized education, we have learned anatomy and physiology, the techniques of physical and pelvic examinations of the nonpregnant women, normal antepartum (before labor and childbirth) care of the pregnant woman, the principles of communication and teaching, the methods of prepared childbirth, normal patterns of labor and delivery and their management, abnormal patterns and ways of detecting them, examination and care of the newborn, postpartum (after delivery) care, medical and obstetric complications of the reproductive cycle, as well as family planning (contraception) and gynecology.

Each student must have put in an average of 500 hours of clinical practice; performed a minimum of 20 deliveries—though most of us have done many more—and assisted with more than that; conducted at least 20 first visits of pregnant patients and at least 100 revisits during pregnancy; and made at least 20 newborn examinations.

When we are ready to practice midwifery, we have had a *minimum* of six years of specialized training: four years in an accredited school of nursing, one year or more of job experience, and at least one year or more of midwifery education in small, highly individualized classes.

At this point, we must then pass a rigorous national examination prepared by the American College of Nurse-Midwives before applying for a license or permit to practice in whatever state we choose.

According to Joyce Beebe, director of the Columbia University Graduate Program in Maternity Nursing and Nurse-Midwifery at Columbia-Presbyterian Medical Center in New York, midwifery students receive exactly the same training in obstetrics as medical students, with the added advantage of having had *much more* clinical experience.

I have gone into all this detail to show that certified nurse-midwifes are very different from Great-aunt Kate and from all the lay midwives who have recently appeared on the scene. We are top-level professionals with medically sound education and experience.

3

History

Throughout history, women have always helped other women deliver their babies. In most other countries they still do—the U.S. is the only place in the world in which midwives have *ever* been outlawed. Midwives deliver about 80 percent of the babies born in the world, in the most highly technological and sophisticated nations as well as in the developing countries.

Though midwives have been in almost total disrepute here until recently, and our American babies have been delivered in the most "scientific" manner ever devised, the infant-mortality rate in the U.S. is significantly higher than in many countries that rely heavily on midwives who are strictly regulated and carefully trained. Sweden and Finland, the Netherlands, Japan, Iceland, and Norway, countries that utilize the services of midwives, have the lowest death rates, according to latest figures (1974) of the United Nations Office of Statistics, followed by France, Denmark, Switzerland, Luxembourg, Spain, Canada, England and Wales, East Germany, Byelorussia, and New Zealand. The

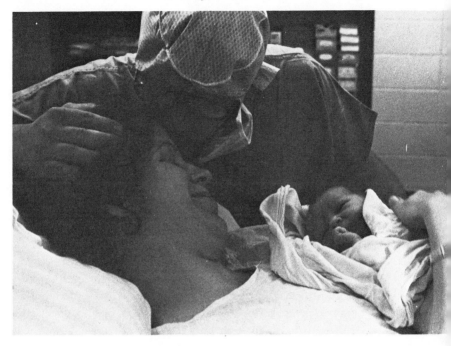

U.S. is seventeenth on the list, along with Australia and Singapore.

In Europe, for many centuries, and in the early days of America, too, lay midwives were the people who practiced obstetrics. They were respected people in their communities because they were the specialists in childbirth. Schools for midwives were set up in many European countries in the eighteenth and nineteenth centuries, and the training and practice of midwifery eventually came to be supervised and controlled by the governments.

In this nation, midwives delivered the babies until the late nineteenth century when obstetrics rapidly became a recognized medical specialty and male physicians began to take over the care of pregnant women. Mortality rates for both mothers and babies were appallingly high at that time, and the doctors began urging women to have their children in hospitals in which "modern" techniques such as forceps and anesthesia could be used. Though hospitals in those days were places for the seriously ill and dying, and the physicians knew little, if any, more than experienced lay midwives, women soon became convinced hospitals were the safest places for them to give birth.

Before long, the granny midwives in America, especially the old-country midwives who arrived with the waves of immigrants flocking to the New World, fell into utter disrepute. Blamed for the shocking mortality statistics, they were quickly forced out of business.

In 1905, more than 40 percent of the babies born in New York City were delivered by midwives. In 1906, the New York City Health Department scathingly denounced midwives, and by 1932 only about 10 percent of all babies delivered in New York City arrived with the help of the grannies. This trend continued despite the fact that the city had opened, in 1911, the country's first school of midwifery, the Bellevue School, to train and control midwives. The school closed in 1936.

Midwives rapidly became a phenomenon of the past, as more and more states began to condemn and outlaw them except in the most remote rural areas. Obstetrics became the province of the doctors—and therefore men.

But although the midwives were banned, and childbirth had been taken over by the male medical Establishment in the U.S., midwives continued to flourish in every other part of the world. And even here, the idea of women caring for women during a thoroughly female happening in their lives never really disappeared.

Before long, midwives—and women—began to make a comeback in America, until now, once again, we are respected deliverers of health care. We're not the same as the granny midwives because we are highly educated and function as professionals, intensively trained in maternal and perinatal health care, but we are, like the best of the grannies, competent, concerned, female, empathetic, involved, family-oriented.

There are still not very many of us—about 1,800 certified nurse-midwives in January 1976. But that's a big jump from the 1960s when there were only a few hundred. In only the last five years, membership in our professional organization, the American College of Nurse-Midwives, has grown from 589 to 1,011 (1975), with 619 of these midwives in active practice and 165 in training.

The first stirrings of rekindled belief in midwives was evidenced in the early 1920s when the Maternity Center Association of New York, an organization of lay volunteers, physicians, and nurses, whose purpose was to upgrade maternity care through education, proposed that the Bellevue School start to train *nurses* as midwives. The suggestion was turned down by the city health department.

So, modern midwifery began in the hills of Kentucky. In 1925, Mary Breckinridge, already a graduate public-health nurse, came home from England where she had attended an accredited midwifery school, and started the Frontier Nursing Service's midwifery program. She imported other English-educated nurse-midwives and encouraged many American nurses to seek advanced training in England. By providing first-rate care for the mountain people, she spurred the movement in this country.

The first school in America for nurse-midwifery, the Lobenstine Clinic, was set up in New York in 1932 with the help of a nurse-midwife who was loaned by the Frontier Nursing Service. This was later called the Maternity Center Association School, and its graduates provided home deliveries. The Frontier Nursing Service followed with its own school in 1939.

In 1958, the Maternity Center Association School was transferred to Downstate Medical Center-Kings County Hospital in New York, to become the first midwifery program in a major U.S. municipal or county hospital with a

university affiliation. Dr. Louis Hellman, chief of obstetrics, who recognized the need for better maternity care, was the architect of this program.

Dr. Hellman, a leader in the development of midwifery programs, felt and often expressed the opinion that midwives were the wave of the future. After World War II, there was a boom in births, the number of physicians going into obstetrics was declining, and obstetric residents were becoming scarce. Who would deliver all the expected babies? Dr. Hellman, who knew that midwives could easily handle most births, thought they were the answer for our overtaxed maternity services.

Other schools for midwifery were established, at first slowly and then after the early front-runners, at a rapid rate. Currently, there are 15 schools in the U.S. offering midwifery programs.

New Mexico, in 1945, was the first place to pass a law concerning nurse-midwives and to allow them to be licensed. New York City was the next, but not until 1959. In the meantime, four years earlier, the American College of Nurse-Midwives was organized to set standards, provide guidelines, and offer accreditation to educational programs.

A handful of New York City hospitals soon allowed midwives to deliver babies in their clinics, but only for training purposes. It wasn't until 1964, when Roosevelt Hospital recruited me, that nurse-midwives were ever permitted to practice as specialists in voluntary hospitals.

One of the important roadblocks to our progress was the strenuous resistance to us by many physicians and nurses who were adamant adherents of traditional childbirth methods or who felt that only doctors could do this job properly. When we first came into the hospitals, few doctors and nurses, as well as the rest of the staff, had ever seen a midwife before. (One obstetrics resident told me he expected I'd be an elderly lady with a bottle of herbs in my back pocket.) Some felt midwifery was a step backward to

the early days of medicine. Others viewed us as threats to
their egos—we represented change in their traditional patterns of practice. Many physicians felt—and still do—that
midwives posed an economic threat, that we represented
competition and would take patients away from them.

Often nurses have felt that midwives stepped between
them and the doctors. Obstetric nurses have always been
the doctors' chief assistants and stand-ins, frequently delivering babies themselves when the babies insisted on arriv-

ing before the doctors came. Now *we* appeared, and the nurses were assisting us as well. What nurses are beginning to realize, however, is that the team approach provides the best maternity care—and many of our nurses have gone on to become midwives themselves.

The midwives at Roosevelt were spared much of this natural resentment because we did not come into an existing obstetrics department with routines that had become petrified over the years. I was hired and started work when the obstetrics department opened its doors, so that I did not have to fight an already existing system and was actually able to initiate new, progressive, family-centered childbirth procedures. The obstetricians at Roosevelt gave us complete support, and the nursing supervisor as well as the staff nurses have been totally cooperative. But midwives in other hospitals have spent months or even years in their efforts to become accepted members of the team. Many have found it impossible, because of opposition from doctors, to become accredited to deliver in some institutions.

> *"My husband and I had seen three or four obstetricians before we came here. I wanted the feeling that the doctor, my husband, and I would all be working together. I didn't want to feel like a patient. Because my father's a doctor, I felt I should have one, but they were so paternal, and I didn't think they were enthusiastic about my ideas. After the fourth try, we came here. I was really impressed the first visit, which lasted an hour. My husband came with me, and we decided, yes, this was the place."*

Gradually, however, physicians and hospitals are discovering, from the example we and other midwives are setting, that nurse-midwives can share their load of work, provide excellent care, give them more time to pursue their specialties and interests, and actually attract patients. For example, we have drawn many women to our midwifery program who wouldn't have come to our hospital normally.

The hospital benefits because of the additional patients, and the doctors benefit when we transfer patients to them or require their services for the mother or baby.

The single event that gave midwifery its major push toward real acceptance by the medical profession was a joint statement, 10 years in the making, issued in 1971 by the American College of Obstetricians and Gynecologists, their nurses association, and the American College of Nurse-Midwives. The statement declared that, as part of a medically directed team, "qualified nurse-midwives may assume responsibility for the complete care and management of uncomplicated maternity patients." With this momentous endorsement, midwives officially became part of the mainstream of health care in this country.

From that moment, we began to truly flourish. Government and foundation money found its way into the movement, federal agencies recognized us, and state laws began to change.

At this writing, only five states—Massachusetts, Michigan, Alabama, Missouri, and Wisconsin—have restrictive laws prohibiting nurse-midwives from practicing. Because licensing and practice are controlled by the individual states, however, there are nearly as many laws as there are states. Some states have passed laws allowing midwifery; others have no laws dealing with the matter; and still others have ambiguous laws that can be interpreted in a variety of ways.

While the state-by-state situation is not completely clear at this time, and many communities are considering changes in their legislation or are coming up with new interpretations of existing law, the fact remains that nurse-midwifery is firmly established and on its way to becoming a widely accepted profession.

4

The Roosevelt Story
. . . and Others

When I was hired in 1964 by Roosevelt (a 600-bed voluntary hospital) to help with the clinic load, I was virtually the only nurse-midwife in the entire U.S. whose job was to manage pregnancies and deliver babies (except for a few nurse-midwives who worked in two city hospitals in New York and with the Frontier Nursing Service in Kentucky). Later, my colleagues and I became the first midwives ever to set up an autonomous midwifery service to which private patients could come just as they would to an obstetrician.

Before becoming a midwife, I was head nurse of labor and delivery at Columbia-Presbyterian Medical Center. I later moved to New York Hospital. One day, Dr. Ralph Gause, who was an attending physician at New York Hospital, cut the cord of a baby he had just delivered, turned to me, and asked: "Why do we need doctors to handle normal deliveries? With some specialized training, you could do it just as well." It was a casual conversation, but it changed my life.

I made an appointment at the Maternity Center Association to inquire about midwifery training. Intrigued by what I discovered, I resigned from my job and enrolled in the Center's new program at Downstate Medical Center at Kings County Hospital in Brooklyn, one of only three midwifery training programs then existing.

When I finished (among the first graduates of the school), there was no job for me as a professional midwife unless I wanted to teach or do family planning or parent education—or leave the country for missionary work. I accepted an internship at Kings County for a year, then learned that Dr. Gause was becoming Director of a brand-new obstetric service being set up at Roosevelt Hospital—now an affiliate of Columbia-Presbyterian Medical Center—and wanted a midwife on his staff. A quick interview, and I was hired; I had become a pioneer, though I didn't realize it.

At that time, the birth rate was soaring, and we ran a very busy department. In my first years at the hospital, I delivered hundreds of babies on the clinic service, working along with the attending physicians and the residents. I taught normal obstetrics to medical students as well. As the patient load grew larger, we gradually increased our midwives to five. I loved my job, alternated deliveries with the residents, and in fact performed more deliveries than any of them because I was so eager to work.

It was the perfect start for me and the basis for our eventual private service. In fact, I think it was the only way it could have happened. Most of the doctors affiliated with the hospital had never seen, or perhaps even heard of, a nurse-midwife before. They, too, I'm sure, thought we were the ragged remnants of the Dark Ages or simply nurses with inflated egos and delusions of grandeur. But the way I and later my colleagues performed soon convinced them of our worth. We became very much respected by the attending physicians as well as the house staff and were often specially requested to tend to their patients when they were not available. They felt secure with us, as they gradually discovered that we were truly competent.

Over the next number of years, however, the birth rate began to plummet at our hospital as well as at every other in the nation. The "pill" and the new abortion laws, along with the recession, brought about a marked trend toward small, planned families. Obstetric departments in many institutions became underutilized. We wondered how we were going to survive.

In the meantime, Dr. Gause retired, and we had a new director of obstetrics, Dr. Thomas Dillon, who came to us from New York Hospital. Dr. Dillon, like his predecessor, gave us tremendous support, and he, too, took a big gamble on midwives. He decided on an experiment, something that had never been tried before in this country.

The experiment was to set up, on a trial basis, a private midwifery service. We five midwives would be able to accept private patients who would come to us just as they would to an obstetrician, following them from their first prenatal visits through their deliveries—if all proceeded normally. If all went smoothly, the women would never have to see a physician. But, as part of the hospital team, we would be backed up by the board-certified obstetricians/gynecologists on the staff who would take over the patients if we—the midwives—decided there was any risk.

> *"I never thought, 'Wait a minute, she's not a doctor.' She obviously knew what she was doing."*

We all felt the time was right—the mood was being set for this service. Women were beginning to ask questions about what was happening to their bodies, and parent education was becoming very popular. We recognized that there probably was a large group of middle-income, well-educated, well-informed women in the New York area who wanted their normal pregnancies to be treated like normal, natural physiological events, who wanted some control over what was happening to them, who wanted to go through the childbirth experience with another woman, and who were

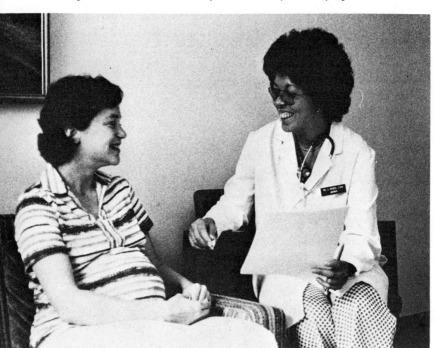

resisting the despotism of the usual hospital procedures common in America.

Add to all that, of course, the fact that, with the drop in the birth rate, most hospitals were having difficulty filling up maternity beds. Maybe establishing a private midwifery service was an intelligent way to provide a needed service and bring patients our way.

As Dr. Dillon says, "We took a chance. We knew there were a lot of women out there who were looking for a different kind of treatment, we knew there had been a noticeable increase in home births among women who were rejecting the usual methods of delivering babies, and we strongly felt there was a need for care that would combine the empathy of a woman-to-woman relationship, enlightened consumerism, prepared childbirth, and self-determination with the modern medical techniques only a hospital setting can provide. We sympathized with the woman who wanted out of the impersonal dehumanizing atmosphere of the sterile hospital, but we knew with certainty that she might just need the technology the medical establishment had come up with in recent years.

"In 1974, we didn't know what our midwives could or should do. We didn't know if we were embarking on an experiment that would fall on its face or become a booming success, or neither. I'd say we're halfway through our great experiment, and so far it has been nothing less than spectacular."

With the go-ahead from Dr. Dillon, we went to work, trying to achieve the right blend of inspiration and practicality. Our midwifery service is located in the hospital, but because in the majority of cases we would not need the doctors, the anesthesia, blood banks, and operating rooms, we tried to play down the hospital atmosphere and create a more relaxed environment. We encouraged 24-hour rooming in and the active participation of the fathers in the labor and delivery rooms and allowed the unrestricted use of cameras for the birth of their child. We emphasized our flexibility and our willingness to give our women what they were looking for in the childbirth experience.

We set our fee—a package price that included everything from the first prenatal visit through the delivery, two days in the hospital, and a postpartum checkup—at the lowest possible amount (it was then $459; now it is $899). This, of course, has proved to be one of our attractions; the usual price of childbirth today is astronomical, ranging from $1,200 to $2,000.

We sent out 500 announcement cards and a press release and started out with one morning a week set aside for prenatal and postpartum visits. We continued to manage clinic pregnancies and deliveries as always while we waited to see what would happen.

What happened was an explosion. Our staff and attending physicians sent us patients; we acquired some from among the clinic population, others from the relatives and friends of the hospital staff. After our first deliveries, CBS News found us, then the other networks and radio stations, magazines, and newspapers. In a very short time, we reached the quota of patients we thought we should handle in this experimental program and had to turn away hundreds of others, who were often bitterly disappointed.

We also turned away many potential patients who did not meet our very rigid criteria of "normal." If there was any reason to believe that a woman might not have a normal birth—and this was left to our judgment alone—we did not accept her into our program.

The five of us now see patients three mornings and one afternoon a week, deliver all our own private patients, and still perform 35 percent of the normal, spontaneous clinic deliveries. In addition, we teach both medical students and nurse-midwifery students from Columbia University.

Some of our new patients today are having a baby the second time around with us or are coming to us on the recommendation of their friends or relations who have had their babies here.

The midwives are present or on call around the clock, and there is constant medical coverage by the obstetricians on the hospital staff. We explain to all our new patients that because there are five midwives, and all of us are not on duty all of the time, we cannot guarantee that a specific one of us will deliver their babies. But by the time they have come for all of their prenatal visits, they will have met and gotten to know each of us well.

> "I went to a woman ob-gyn who's given up deliveries. She told me to look into the midwifery service here. I couldn't believe it. But she said, 'Go and talk, and come back if you don't like it. I'll find you another doctor.' I talked, and I stayed, and I am so happy I did."

In the first two years of our private practice, 247 babies were born to our own patients. A total of 88.6 percent, or 219 of these, were natural, spontaneous deliveries, including nine vaginal breech deliveries and four sets of twins. Of that total, 4.8 percent were transferred to the care of obstetricians for forceps deliveries because of fetal distress or a prolonged second stage of labor. And 6.4 percent required cesarean sections by physicians because of complicated breech presentation, face presentation, or disproportion of baby to pelvis. These percentages are considerably lower than those of the clinic population or even those of private obstetricians, partly because our patients are so carefully screened.

During pregnancy, 14 of our patients had spontaneous abortions, and 15 patients we had accepted were transferred out to physicians because their progress was not considered completely normal. Some of the reasons for transfers were hypertension, toxemia, asthma, superficial thrombophlebitis, heart murmurs, and abnormal glucose tolerance tests.

All mothers have done well; however, we had one infant mortality because of congenital deformity, another because of prematurity, and one stillbirth at 5½ months.

The hospital, for the first time in many years, delivered over 2,000 babies in 1975. It was partly because of the midwives' contribution and partly because Roosevelt was becoming known as a hospital (and I like to think we were a big influence) in which the patients were allowed to have their babies pretty much as they wanted to. All obstetric patients may be accompanied right into the delivery room by their husbands or anyone else they choose, are encouraged to deliver spontaneously, may have rooming-in, all-day visiting by the father of the baby, as well as an early discharge.

Our group of midwives could have handled more patients than we did in those first two years, but we wanted to begin slowly and cautiously so that we could be certain our program was working. And we did not want to become so

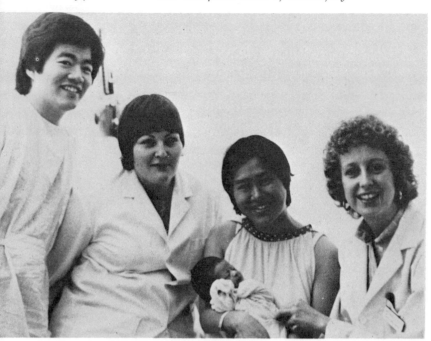

rushed, as many obstetricians have, that we would dilute our services. Gradually, we will increase our load until we reach the optimum number economically, medically, and psychologically.

> "I consider myself a first-class citizen, and I demand first-class care. I won't accept assembly-line treatment anymore. I don't want a quick poke, a stethoscope on my belly, a blood-pressure bandage on my arm, and then good-by. I want somebody who'll be interested in me, an individual with individual problems, somebody who will listen to me and talk to me. Well, I found that person, five of them, as a matter of fact. Those midwives seem really interested."

Our experience here has been an astonishingly accurate weathervane of the acceptance of midwives in the country. As soon as we started the private service in 1974, and especially after the media discovered us and gave us tremendous amounts of exposure, we were inundated with inquiries and requests for information as well as for deliveries—many more than we could possibly handle.

Women call us from distant places asking where they might find midwives in their parts of the country. We get constant requests for interviews from television studios, magazines, newspapers. Letters and telephone calls from hospitals, as well as from groups of interested parents and other midwives, pour in asking us to tell them how we began our private service and how they might do the same.

The pressure grows daily. Obviously, we five women at Roosevelt Hospital cannot cope with the huge demand, and other programs have already started to share the load, with the result that more and more middle-class women are having their babies delivered by midwives.

> *"It was a very intense experience. I felt everyone was with me. I wouldn't have missed it for anything, even though it was a tough job."*

In New York City, for example, in which nurse-midwifery got its biggest early support, another voluntary hospital has just opened a private service: The Albert Einstein College of Medicine Hospital now has a nurse-midwife who works with a group of private obstetricians and takes her own patients as an equal member of the team. The hospital plans to form a group practice for midwives as well. And before this book is in the bookstores several other metropolitan-area hospitals will have done the same.

Other hospitals in and around New York City have found that their middle-class patient population has noticeably risen in their midwifery-staffed clinics. Brookdale Hospital in Brooklyn, to name one, reports that it is now getting many middle-class patients who could obviously afford private care.

In the meantime, Maternity Center Association's Child-bearing Center has opened its doors on Ninety-second Street in New York. The Center, many years in the planning and the special project of Ruth Lubic, C.N.M., a nurse-midwife who is general director of the Association, is similar in some ways to our program at Roosevelt and a tremendous departure in others.

It is not a hospital, though it has as its back-up facility, Lenox Hill Hospital, 11 minutes away by ambulance. Staffed by five nurse-midwives, three obstetricians, and one pediatrician, the Childbearing Center came about, according to Mrs. Lubic, as an alternative plan for couples considering opting out of hospitals and having a home delivery.

"Do-it-yourself home births are dangerous," says Mrs. Lubic, "but they're a real trend. We're trying to find out if homelike, out-of-hospital but professional maternal care for low-risk patients can be made safe, satisfying, and low-cost. This is a demonstration project, in keeping with the Center's role of promoting better maternity care. We are testing the concept. If it is successful, we will help other centers to get started while we go on to another project. We may also in the process influence hospitals to become more homelike and attuned to patients' desires." Midwives handle the prenatal care and the deliveries, with the obstetricians present or on call. Because the Center is not a hospital, its patients are rigidly screened for normalcy.

Since our midwifery service at Roosevelt is located *in* the hospital, we can handle emergencies immediately and can co-manage occurrences such as births of twins, breeches, and premature rupture of the membranes, which may need stimulation of labor, so that we can maintain continuity of care.

Elsewhere in the country, other midwifery services for the middle-class patient have sprung up over the last few years. Perhaps the best known is Booth Maternity Center, a freestanding maternity hospital, in Philadelphia. Run by the Salvation Army and originally a home for unwed mothers (there is still a residence program for single parents), this hospital, with its team of midwives and physicians, serves a cross section of the childbearing population of Philadelphia today. Says nurse-midwife Kitty Ernst, "Most of our patients today can afford to go elsewhere, but they have chosen us. They come because they like the way they're treated here. We're family-centered and feel that childbirth should be a confident, joyous occasion, with the patients taking part in every decision that concerns them." Booth delivered over 1,000 babies in 1975, up from 279 in 1971, despite the declining birth rate.

Springfield and Clark County Hospital in Springfield, Ohio, is a community hospital whose patients are from all strata of society. A team of seven midwives delivers all patients if their pregnancies and births proceed normally. Back-up physicians take over high-risk cases. In 1975, they handled about 700 deliveries.

In Minneapolis, at the University of Minnesota, four midwives run their own service within the department of obstetrics, contracting with patients for their maternity care. This last year, because of the midwifery program, deliveries at the hospital have tripled. A special feature of the Minnesota program is the formation of support groups of couples who meet weekly with each other before and after their babies arrive.

Hennepin County Medical Center, also in Minneapolis, has a staff of midwives who see their own patients, delivering them in special birthing rooms outfitted with double beds, lounge chairs, and private bathrooms. In 1975, the midwives here delivered about 20 babies a month.

In many other communities, obstetrician/midwife teams have gone into private practice—in my opinion the ideal arrangement. With more residents now working with midwives in the hospitals, more will be looking for midwives to go into practice with them so that they will have time to devote to the complicated obstetric cases as well as to gynecology. Each team works in its own individual way. In some cases, the midwives provide most of the prenatal and postpartum care, but no deliveries. In others, midwives manage all the normal cases, including deliveries. In still others, they teach parent-education classes as well. In Americus, Georgia, a team of doctors and midwives serves a population area of 88,000. And a team of two doctors and two midwives operates in Eugene, Oregon. There are several team practices in Connecticut; more in West Virginia, Maryland, Florida, South Carolina, and many other states.

Some of the most interesting midwifery programs exist in the military. Obstetrics is one of the busiest branches of medicine in military hospitals, coinciding with a perennial and growing shortage of specializing physicians, now that doctors are no longer drafted. Midwives, therefore, are gradually becoming a permanent feature.

The U.S. Air Force was the first military service to use midwives to deliver its babies and has the largest and most impressive program. Under the direction of Johanna Borsellega, who was one our first midwives at Roosevelt Hospital, the Air Force, which already had many midwives in its hospitals, established its own school of midwifery in 1973 at the Malcolm Grow Medical Center at Andrews Air Force Base, Maryland. The school, affiliated with the Georgetown University School of Nursing, was founded after a careful study of all the possible ways of compensating for the doctor shortage.

In October 1975, there were 40 midwives on active duty in 16 Air Force hospitals, including one in England, delivering approximately 1,100 babies in 1974. Although officially members of the nurse corps, they are responsible to the base chief of ob/gyn in each hospital.

The U.S. Army Medical Department at Fort Knox, Kentucky, started off with one midwife at Ireland Army Base in

September 1972. Today there are 16 nurse-midwives at three Army bases, with four Army nurses taking midwifery training at the University of Kentucky. In 1975, the midwives delivered 453 babies.

The Navy, which has one nurse-midwife at Pensacola Naval Air Station, plans to train career navy nurses in civilian schools.

5

The Women Who
Come to Us

The women who come to us as private patients at Roosevelt Hospital are, with very few exceptions, extremely well informed about pregnancy and childbirth. They have thoroughly studied the subject, and they usually know exactly how they want to have their babies. They are people who shop around for the services they want; many have seen several doctors before they come to us, have investigated hospitals, and some have even considered having their babies at home. They are not the kind of people who fall into the nearest doctor's office or simply go to an obstetrician recommended by a neighbor. They are fully aware of all the options available to them, from hospital clinics to private obstetricians, and they are looking for something more than the classic doctor-patient relationship.

Again, with few exceptions, their pregnancies have been planned, and they are going to have only one, two, or maybe three children. Most (59 percent) are having their first.

Most of our mothers-to-be are in their late twenties or

early thirties (the average age is 29). They are often career women who, for educational, professional, or personal reasons, have postponed their pregnancy till later than the conventional age for childbearing.

As a group, they are very well educated, usually with college degrees. Many are professionals. We've had doctors, including two pediatricians, among our private patients, along with several doctors' wives, a number of nurses, lawyers, teachers, psychologists, and counselors. Some have interrupted their careers to stay home with their children, but I have found that most of these women pursue some kind of work at home. The others go back to jobs right away or after a few months.

The majority of our patients who have had previous children were delivered by obstetricians, but a few who were living in other countries used midwives. Two were former clinic patients who were delivered, by chance, by midwives.

The women who come to us are people who usually could and would manage to afford the $1,500 or $2,000 they'd need to pay for an obstetrician and hospital stay if they had to. They are not the kind of women who would ordinarily choose to go to a clinic. We've found that only a few have selected us for economic reasons, though the low fee for our service certainly is an added attraction.

> *"I went to ____ Hospital for my initial clinic visit. I was shuffled around from one place to another and was left sitting on a bench for over an hour. I left in tears and never went back. When you're pregnant, you want it to be as nice as possible."*

Many, if not most, of them have gone to physicians for their initial visits, talked to others at length, and closely questioned their friends and acquaintances about their experiences. They've read every book that's been printed on pregnancy and childbirth, and they've thought about what they want—and don't want. When they come to us, they have usually come for philosophical reasons. They want what we have to give them—even if it means doing battle with their families. I remember one doctor's daughter who was delivered by us—he couldn't believe that *his* daughter was going to a midwife, especially since one of the obstetricians, one of "the best" in the city, at his own hospital would have delivered her free, out of professional courtesy. One patient was telling me about her conversations with her mother, who had been told her daughter was seeing the midwives. "Dear, I know you've been to the midwife, but when are you going to see the doctor?"

Our patients have been a very healthy group who have

taken good care of their bodies—about which they have a very positive feeling, pregnant or not. They want them to be treated with respect and with dignity.

Many of our patients come to us because they demand empathy and feel this is more readily forthcoming from another woman. Very few of them have been militant feminists—though some are—but merely feel that women will understand them better, feel for them more, be more caring about their bodies and their babies. They think midwives will be more interested in their small complaints and minor questions. Because we are women, too, they can relax with us, knowing that we will empathize and identify.

> *"I like women more for some things. You get the feeling they're really interested and they're going to take care of you like a friend. Barbara said to me, 'Every time a baby is born, I am thrilled.' And I believe it. It was like she was part of the family."*

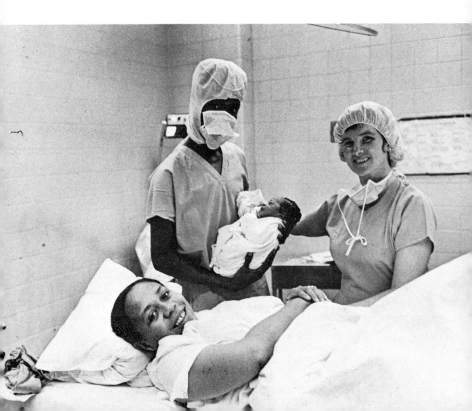

They seek the sense of warmth they can get by talking to another woman about something quite normal and female that's happening to them. Many of our patients have told us they deliberately sought out a woman.

And our women want attention, a lot of attention. They don't want to feel like they're on an assembly line, pushed through a system they have no control over. They want someone with them during labor. They want enough time to ask every question that's come to them in the middle of the night and to get a leisurely and complete answer. They don't want to be treated like children and won't put up with a "Let me take care of it, I'm the expert" approach. They are looking for personalized treatment.

> *"The midwives take a lot of time with you, right from the beginning. None of the office visits lasted less than a half hour, and I asked them dumb questions, which they answered very seriously, questions I'd never ask a male doctor. They never hurry you. My husband went with me to every checkup, and I even brought my four-year-old a few times. He loved listening to the baby's heartbeat."*

Perhaps, most of all, the women who seek out the services of a nurse-midwife are demanding their rights. They are demanding to be full partners in this whole miraculous event. And we want them to be. They want to know what is going on all the time, what their bodies are doing and what is being done to their bodies. They want to be treated as intelligent people who can help make the decisions that so vitally concern them and their babies, not to be intimidated by "the system." They want to assume control over what happens to them, to hold on to their identities, to be treated not as a sick or wounded person but as one who is going through a perfectly normal process and is basically going to be doing the job of giving birth herself.

Our patient wants to have her own baby. Herself. And as long as everything proceeds normally, she can. But she's not the kind of woman who would go out into the fields to deliver her infant, nor would she feel it was worth the risk to have it at home with only friends around to help. She wants the presence of a specialist who has had good training, can spot difficulties if any arise, and can guide, reassure, and support her while she has her own baby.

The woman who chooses us here at Roosevelt Hospital feels safer having her baby in a hospital. There has been a trend, which seems to be growing steadily stronger, toward home births. Most home births today, especially in California where the boom is biggest, are attended by lay midwives with no formal training, though some are conducted by certified nurse-midwives and/or physicians. Though I personally know of none that have been mismanaged, I feel strongly that the *hospital* is the right place to deliver babies.

Some of our patients have told us they had originally wanted home births because, after all, what better setting for such a family event than the warmth of the home as opposed to the coldness, the bareness, the sterility of a hospital? I understand their desires completely, and I contend that the risks are not worth it.

All of our patients want to have their babies in as natural a way as possible. They all attend parent-education classes—we insist that they do—and they learn how to help themselves give birth. They want as little outside intervention as possible—no drugs, no episiotomies (surgical incisions to enlarge the vaginal opening), no forceps, no shaves or enemas, no inductions. They know it's best for the baby and their emotional attachment to it to hold and perhaps nurse the baby immediately right on the delivery table. Some, having read Dr. Leboyer's famous new book, want the lights in the delivery room dimmed.

"She stayed with me from the beginning to the end. I had my other two children with doctors, and once the doctor didn't ever get to the labor room."

They especially don't want to be alone while they labor. They want to have their husbands (or another person who's close to them) with them every moment in the labor room and in the delivery room. They know that the midwife will be with them constantly from the beginning to the end.

They look for hospitals that permit all these things, as well as rooming-in with their babies, and they want to be allowed to go home as quickly as possible.

For all these reasons, our patients have chosen midwives to manage their pregnancies, labors, and deliveries. They have discovered, through their friends or perhaps the media, sometimes through gynecologists and other physicians, that midwives want them to have their babies in the very same way.

> *"They never say no. They do what you want if they can. I'm a vegetarian, and I take no drugs. I told them, don't offer me anything, and talk me out of it if I weaken. And that's what happened. I didn't really need it."*

6

Hospitals Versus Home

More than a few of our private midwifery patients have come to us after seriously considering having their babies at home. Midwives represent to them a compromise between a "warm, family-oriented" home birth and the traditional hospital delivery, which they see as cold and impersonal. I am thankful they did not decide on a home birth, not for our sake but for their own; any midwife who has done enough obstetrics knows that a delivery can only be called absolutely perfectly normal *after it's all over* and the baby is out, crying and healthy. Until that point, there's no way of being certain that everything is going to be completely smooth 100 percent of the time. There is *no way* to guarantee it to anyone.

Though the vast majority of births are normal and simple, there is always a small risk that the particular birth in question won't be; for that reason, only a few nurse-midwives will deliver babies at home. We want to know, and you should, too, that there's a doctor available, a blood bank downstairs, anesthesia at the head of the table, an operating room, and an intensive-care nursery down the hall, though we rarely need to resort to them. If a patient doesn't need any of these things, I'll barricade the doors and fend them off with my life, but it's important to know they're out there just in case. When something goes wrong in childbirth, it can happen very fast.

The trend toward having babies at home as our grandmothers did is definitely growing in America today. The trend began in California among the counterculture groups several years ago and has spread into the East and among middle-income families. Many home births are do-it-yourself affairs with fathers and friends attending or with lay midwives who are usually self-taught.

Because of the demand, physicians and nurse-midwives in some communities are also delivering babies at home. Of course, there have been many successful home births. And if families choose to opt out of the system, they will. People who choose home births are making a statement; they are denouncing hospitals because they don't like what's going on in them. But they must realize that home delivery can be a very risky business. In most Western European nations, the majority of normal deliveries are managed at home, but there are extensive systems of trained midwives and traveling obstetric flying squads, mobile units that can be summoned immediately to provide blood or perform surgery in an emergency. In this country, a woman whose birth suddenly becomes complicated must be taken to a hospital, often too many traffic jams or miles away for comfort.

In spite of my years in the medical Establishment, I am very sympathetic to women who don't want to get involved with cold, inconsiderate, dehumanized hospitals. I understand their desire to share the miraculous experience with the father of the baby and friends, to go back to days that were simpler and more natural, to be free of the "system" and its rules and regulations. And I certainly sympathize with their wish not to have to pay thousands of dollars to have a baby.

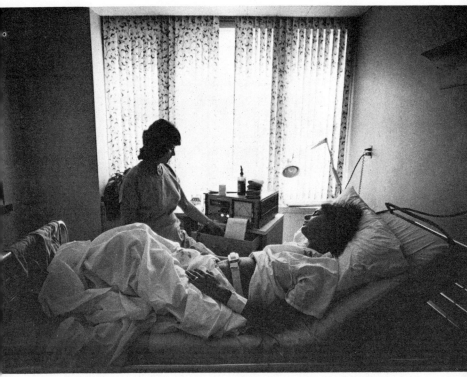

Photo by Alan Perlman

But the risk is too high. It can be dangerous to have a baby at home. A few minutes can make the difference between a baby that is damaged and a baby that is normal and healthy. Just as an example, a baby with respiratory distress syndrome would need the facilities of hospital equipment for resuscitation, as well as the quick attention of a neonatologist. Or the mother may need special care if, for instance, she has severe postpartum hemorrhaging because the uterus does not contract immediately after delivery. Oxytocins, which help the uterus to contract, or perhaps even blood transfusions might be needed.

Still, some couples will just not find hospitals suitable to them in any way, shape, or form and are willing to take the risk and gamble that everything will go well. And some women will want the most expensive obstetrician and the most expensive hospital they can find and insist on being knocked out cold so they won't know a thing about it. They are certainly free to make either choice, but both, in my opinion, are not without hazards.

Much wiser, I think, is our approach, which combines the best of both worlds: a childbirth as natural as it can possibly be, managed by professional midwives in a hospital with extremely flexible rules and the reassurance that, if they're needed, all the resources of a modern institution are available.

My own feeling is that the hospital is the safest place to have a baby. And that hospitals, because of the new demands of women who want childbirth returned to them, must change. If they don't change, the women won't put up with them. Many institutions realized the demand early and have already made tremendous strides toward becoming more homelike and relaxed—with the help, I have to add, of the midwives, who initiated *many* of the changes. And these are the hospitals whose obstetrics units are the busiest today.

I think even these hospitals will have to change still more to restore the feeling of home to childbirth. They must become cozier and warmer and eliminate the most obvious trappings of cold, sterile science. They must be places in which women can bring their own belongings, their other children if they want, their stereos and records, where they can feel easy and relaxed.

Ideally, we envision a separate area for our midwifery patients, furnished in a comfortable, homelike way and allowing for enormous flexibility for the couple—*but* connected by only one door to the hospital's delivery rooms and all the technology we may possibly need.

While the numbers of home births will probably continue to rise in the immediate future, I do not believe that they will ever become a true alternative for very many women.

As Dr. Katherine Kendall, chief of the U.S. Children's Bureau, has said, "Certainly it seems unlikely that there will soon be a mass return to nature . . , and that returning to home deliveries will be the desired alternate answer to the need for improved quality of care . . ."

Ninety-nine percent of American women will continue to check into a hospital for childbirth, with more and more of them choosing the particular hospital and the person who cares for them throughout pregnancy and delivery with more and more discrimination. Those who choose home births must do so knowing all the risks as well as the joys.

7

What Midwives Give

Childbirth in America has begun to change radically in the last few years, and midwives—though I'm sure few of us have ever thought of ourselves as revolutionaries—have had much to do with that change.

Because we are *ourselves*—women trained to help other women give birth as easily and happily and normally as possible—we have helped to humanize "the system," to make it more responsive to the needs and wishes of real people, each of whom is different from the next. By doing what we do, we've been able to demonstrate that joy can be a major part of childbirth. There are still few of us, but we're in strategic positions in hospitals and the community, and we have managed to influence maternity care to a remarkable degree just by being totally flexible ourselves, letting our patients have it their way whenever we can, persuading our tradition-bound hospitals to bend their rigid rules, and turning out beautiful, healthy babies for mothers who tell the world about their happy experiences.

"I didn't want some patronizing doctor to say to me, 'You must let me take care of everything.' I wanted to know exactly what was going on—after all, it's my body and my baby, right?"

On the other hand, changes in childbirth methods have helped to bring about the renascence of the midwife in the U.S. Though many doctors and many hospitals still heavily sedate mothers, bar their husbands from the labor and delivery rooms, prefer to keep the patients "out of it" so they can get the job done efficiently and quickly, and take babies away from their mothers except for a few standardized hours till they go home still unfamiliar with each other, the trend in this country is toward a whole new way of having babies. Actually, what we call "the new way" is a return to the way women have had babies always.

The new way is to deliver bright, alert babies to "awake and aware" mothers (to quote my own mentor, the late Dr. Irwin Chabon, an obstetrician who was an attending physician at Roosevelt Hospital and one of the early proponents of "natural" childbirth) who haven't been drugged and who have learned how to participate actively in their labor and delivery. The new way is to invite fathers to join the family, for newborn babies to feel the love of their parents right there in the delivery room. The new way is a partnership with the patient, keeping her informed of every development and every procedure and having her knowledgeable participation in every decision that's made concerning her and her baby.

In recent years, the medical profession—and the women themselves—have learned about the dangers of overintervention in childbirth. Excessive intervention, in the form of heavy drugs or nonindicated use of forceps, induction, etc., has been blamed for many neurologically damaged babies. I think it's most revealing that the March of Dimes gives money each year to midwifery education as a way of helping to prevent birth defects.

Let me quote Dr. G. J. Kloosterman of the Netherlands, an obstetrician who is a midwifery advocate, at an International Confederation of Midwives Congress in 1972: "Many doctors, especially in the technologically developed Western part of the world . . . have a philosophy . . . and that is that we can improve everything, even natural childbirth in a healthy woman. . . . In the majority of all pregnancies and deliveries, interference is unnecessary." Women are beginning to fight excess intervention and opt for health providers, doctors and midwives who promise not to use it.

They have also begun to protest against the inhumane treatment they have had while giving birth and against the routinized and often humiliating procedures they've been subjected to, necessary or not. They've objected to having their questions and concerns brushed off with, "I'm the expert. I know what's best for you," if not in words, then in attitude and action. They have found out, through prepared-childbirth classes, that it is possible, in most instances, to have their babies while remaining in complete control of themselves.

> *"The first time I was pregnant, I was really nervous and scared. I wanted to talk about it with the doctor, but he was so obviously in a hurry that I couldn't even tell him. That was my first visit. The next time, I did say something, and he made some little clucking noises, pressed my shoulder, and told me not to worry about a thing. 'After all,' he said, 'women have always had babies.' The first time I saw the midwife this time around, we spent three-quarters of an hour together, and I got all the support I needed. I felt she understood."*

Additionally, women have started to actively reject the physicians and hospitals that won't give them what they're looking for and to seek out the kind of care they want. Many, because they won't put up with the standard routines and what they consider cold technology, have abandoned hospitals and doctors altogether and are having their babies at home.

"With my first baby, I felt like nobody really cared. I was supposed to do as I was told and not make a fuss about anything. You couldn't ask why; rules were rules. I didn't have any identity."

So it's the women themselves who have discovered the kind of childbirth they want and are beginning to insist on having it. It's the women who say to a doctor or a hospital, "I want to have my baby my way, and if you won't go along, I'll go somewhere else," who have forced obstetrics to change the most. They've questioned every aspect of childbirth and want to know *why* and *how* and if it's to their benefit. The women are the consumers, and they've learned that when they're paying for a service, they should expect the best.

It all corresponds with a trend in the country of no longer accepting the flat dictates of the medical Establishment, whether it concerns having tonsils out, ingesting antibiotics, or producing babies. Women are questioning, probing, comparing, and demanding to know.

"It's the eternal waiting that gets to me. I remember always sitting in that doctor's office for an hour or an hour and a half before my turn came. And twice, after long waits, he was called to the hospital before he got to me."

For all these reasons, many doctors have changed their ways, and hospitals have been forced to provide family-centered, individualized care. They are realizing that although medical science has in recent years greatly improved maternity care and reduced maternal and infant death rates dramatically, it may have gone too far, making women feel unimportant and depersonalized, voiceless, helpless, and demoralized.

Hospitals with midwifery services are attracting patients they would never have seen in their institutions before. At Roosevelt, for instance, we've had midwifery patients who have come to us from 50 miles away and patients who, though residents of New York City, live nowhere near the hospital or even Manhattan and would normally plan to deliver closer to home. We've attracted patients away from suburban obstetricians, suburban hospitals, and conventional care. A hospital in Minneapolis has seen its business triple in the year that it has offered midwifery deliveries.

Though midwives first came into the hospitals because of an impending shortage of obstetricians and a projected baby boom, now we are sought out because women like who we are and what we give.

WE ARE WOMEN: The case for midwifery is really the case for women, for the right to self-determination concerning their bodies. In their search for control over themselves and their lives and for trust in their natural abilities to bear their own babies, women are starting to turn to other women—midwives—who fit neatly into their visions.

They see us as providers of health care, perhaps even as part of the medical Establishment, but also as women who

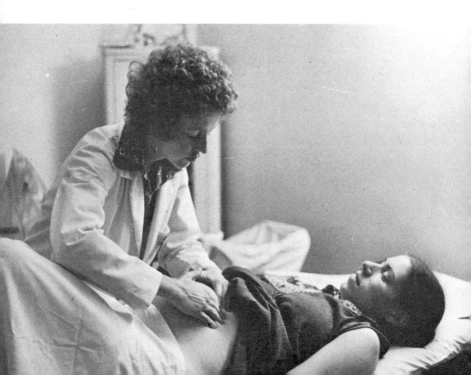

understand their feelings, needs, and hopes. As women, we are kin. We are allies in the struggle to be strong, capable, self-confident, decision-making people.

> *"I feel that a woman can understand me better than a man. You can relax more, tell them more."*

The back-to-nature, back-to-the-simple-life movement has had its impact on our resurgence, too. The trappings of modern life, its artificiality, and its intrusions have made many people feel they have control over only a minor part of their lives. Along with natural foods, moving to the country, blue jeans, and doing your own thing has come a movement toward caring for one's own health needs as much as it is possible. Because midwives are noninterventionists at heart, and because we conceive of childbirth as the woman's function, not technology's, we have been embraced by young people who want to return to the simpler ways of living.

Almost every patient we've ever had in our service has told us that they've felt so much more comfortable and free to be themselves with us. They are not embarrassed to ask personal questions, to expose their fears and their bodies. One woman said to me recently, "You know, it's a silly thing, but this is the first time I've ever had a physical examination when I haven't made sure to shave my legs. I don't have to keep up my image. I can relax much more with you because I'm a woman talking to another woman."

> *"I feel like we're friends, and she treats me like one."*

Women have been trained throughout history to try to please men, to be attractive, charming, and perhaps subservient. They often carry this attitude over to their relationship with their physician and as a consequence don't want to bother him, turn him off, annoy him with "petty" female complaints and insecurities, or let him see them when they are not looking their best. While I am sure that few obstetricians judge their patients on their attractiveness or sexuality, many women can't completely shed their traditional roles and relax. With us, other women, they can be comfortable.

And they know that because we are women, too, we know how it feels to be up in stirrups on an examining table, one of the more undignified positions, and we understand more about a woman's feelings concerning her body than males, who will never get pregnant, have a baby, experience menstrual cramps, or have secret worries about their female reproductive organs. Our bodies are the same as theirs.

> *"I guess I felt good with her because she was a woman. You know she knows what it feels like."*

Many women in the last few years have, for the very same reasons, decided to switch to female obstetricians/gynecologists, but these are unfortunately hard to find. Out of about 18,000 practicing and resident obstetricians in the country today, only about 1,000 are women according to the American College of Obstetricians and Gynecologists. Not only that, but female obstetricians, no doubt *because* they are women, are swamped with patients and so usually have no more time to give than their male counterparts.

Because many busy obstetricians are learning that women are usually more comfortable with other women when they are going through this female experience—and also because they need help in coping with their case loads—more and more of them are bringing (or contemplating doing so) midwives into their private practices so they can work as a team. Drs. T. Schley Gatewood and Richard B. Stewart, two physicians in Americus, Georgia, who employ nurse-

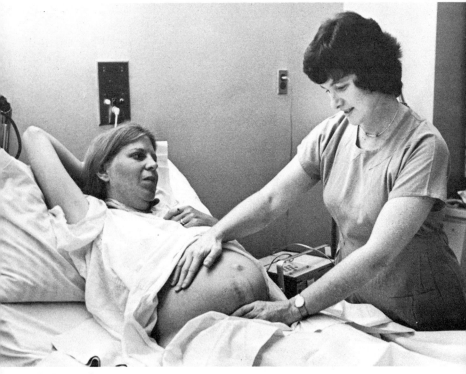

Photo by Suzanne Szasz

midwives, reported on their first year's experience together at a medical conference in 1975. All normal patients had the option of choosing delivery by the obstetricians or the midwives, and 61 percent of the uncomplicated vaginal births were managed by the midwives. The doctors stressed their complete satisfaction with the team operation and stated: "We in the United States must seriously consider adopting the nurse-midwife into our program of obstetric care; we believe that they have much to offer in the total care of the pregnant patient."

WE ARE NOT DOCTORS: It is also partly because we are *not* doctors, who are looked upon with awe in our culture, that midwives come across as friends and helpers rather than patronizing authority figures. Women come to us for guidance because we have more skills than they have in this area, not because they are willing to abdicate their right to have their own babies. Midwives function as advisers, and on our first contact with a patient, we establish a comfortable, friendly, first-name relationship. We build up confidence and an atmosphere of trust and ease—that's just as much a part of our job as performing a pelvic examination.

There has been criticism of midwives from the opposite side of this coin. That we are not doctors has appeal for many women, but others feel we are not *enough* of a departure from the physicians' world. Our critics are the people who feel that hospitals are dehumanizing institutions, that because we are trained in medical centers and work in hospitals, we end up to be "just as bad as the doctors," carbon copies who will fall into the technology all around us, using every machine we can get our hands on and so lose our human touch.

> *"I wanted to have my baby at home. I felt this was my baby, and I wanted him to be born in an atmosphere of love and warmth and peace and quiet. I wanted my husband around and maybe my two-year-old, too. But I couldn't go ahead with it. I couldn't take the chance that something might go wrong. I decided I needed to have the security of the midwives and the hospital."*

The critics mistrust our devotion to "natural" childbirth and the individual needs of each woman because, they say, we have become contaminated by medical thinking. As Suzanne Arm says in her book *Immaculate Deception*, "The nurse-midwife looks and acts much like the physician authority whom she is licensed to assist. She sees life as a doctor does, full of problems, abnormalities and complications, diseases and disorders."

I can only answer the critics by explaining, as I am doing

in this book, exactly how we work and how we think. We have had enough obstetric experience to know that while nature has designed a wonderful and complex process for reproducing ourselves, a process that usually requires little outside interference, scientific research over the years has made it possible to save many mothers and babies who wouldn't make it otherwise. I feel we should use that technological information *when* and *if* we truly need it. But until that time, we must remember to allow nature to perform its own miracles. If we mimic the doctors, I hope we mimic only the positive aspects and maybe do an even better job in human relations.

WE HAVE TIME: We're in no hurry. There are no operating-room schedules we must meet, no gynecologic patients lined up in the office waiting for us, no emergencies we need attend to. We can afford to take all the time we need to talk, and we never want our patients to feel they're infringing on our time. We don't sit behind a desk and shuffle papers as we ask if a patient has any questions. We always sit down next to her and talk as long as she wants, especially during the early prenatal visits when she's usually bursting with questions.

> *"A doctor says to you, do you have any questions, and before you're a quarter down your list, he's standing up and he's gone. My visits with the midwives were the only times I ever came away feeling I really learned something."*

Women want the personalized treatment we give them; they want to sit down and in a relaxed manner discuss their list of queries. Is it okay to go swimming; what about this little pain over here on the left side; should they take iron; what positions are recommended for intercourse; will they have to have an episiotomy; why are they feeling afraid; what will happen when they arrive at the hospital; how will they know if they'll need medication; can their husbands

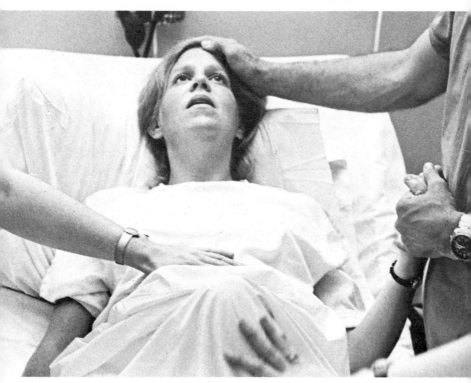

Photo by Suzanne Szasz

stay right there; what does the urinalysis show; is that a
good fetal heartbeat; what if they forget their breathing
techniques when they need them; are they gaining too
much weight; why are they having trouble sleeping; what
will they do with their two-year-old when they have to
come to the hospital? Who will care about all these things?
We do, and we will.

> *"Once you're in the office with the midwife, she never cuts
> you off. She sits down and even volunteers information,
> maybe you'd like to know about this or that. You don't always
> think of everything. Doctors, when the interview is over,
> stand up and shake your hand. Midwives never do that. They
> wait till you stand up."*

Giving our time freely is an especially important part of what midwives give when delivery time comes. We promise our patients that we will stay with them in the labor room from the first moment they arrive at the hospital until after the delivery. Even the most knowledgeable woman, even the woman who has had four babies before, becomes uncertain and sometimes panicked if she's alone in labor. Though the baby's father may be there with her, she still wants the comfort and support of someone whose specialty is childbirth, who knows—and can tell her—exactly what is happening and its implications throughout the whole experience.

> *"When you're in labor, you get scared. You want to be reassured that everything is normal. You start depending on the nurses, who are usually busy with a lot of patients at once, and are so grateful when they pop in on you occasionally. You get to feel you're asking for a big favor every time you ring the bell. My doctor wasn't there when I really needed him."*

Probably the most common complaint I've heard from women who have had unhappy experiences giving birth is that they were left to labor all by themselves in a strange sterile room, attended sporadically by busy nurses and two-minute visits from their obstetricians. Often the doctor has not shown his face at all until a few minutes before the delivery and occasionally has missed the event altogether. Even though about half of the women in the U.S. attend parent-education classes today and learn the techniques that help them cope with their contractions, and even though many hospitals now allow fathers in the labor room, they need the help we can give them. By the time our patient is at term and in labor, she has come to know us and trust us and wants the comfort of our presence. We are there for her alone and she knows it.

"Sometimes I feel I've got to think up some good questions to ask the midwife this visit. I think she'd be disappointed if I didn't."

WE STRESS PREPARED CHILDBIRTH: Having a baby *normally* means having it vaginally and spontaneously. It means heavy drugs are out, and it means the patient must be wide awake and ready to work along with us, staying on top of her contractions and in control of her emotions and her actions. It doesn't mean suffering—we will always offer light medication if a patient wants it. For these reasons, we promote—in fact, insist on—parent-education classes so that she will know everything she can about her pregnancy, the stages of labor, and how to help herself along. We don't want her to have any surprises or underground fears. (For an extended discussion of prepared childbirth see Chapter 8.)

The women who search out midwives today know that we advocate prepared childbirth, and they wouldn't come to us if they wanted it any other way. Occasionally, though, a woman will call us to inquire about our midwifery service and tells us she wants to be "knocked out cold." We tell her she'll have to look elsewhere for that.

"For my first baby, I went to a highly recommended obstetrician. He told me natural childbirth was barbaric. I didn't know any better, and I went along with him. It was awful. He induced the baby, my hands were strapped down, the pain was terrible. Right after he delivered the baby, he left, leaving the nurses to cope with me. It turned out he was going to a convention. With my second pregnancy, I wasn't about to go to a doctor. I'd heard about the midwives here, and from the very first visit with them, I was so happy. They're so involved with you. It was a totally different experience."

We have, of course, delivered some patients who haven't thoroughly prepared themselves for childbirth for one reason or another. Though it's more difficult for them and for us when they haven't learned what to expect and how to deal with their contractions, we are there with them constantly and can lead them along step by step so that they, too, may have a good experience.

WE ARE NONINTERVENTIONISTS: Our orientation is toward childbirth as a normal, natural physiological event, not as a disease or illness. Birth is an event that can take place, 9 times out of 10, without heroic medical measures, usually with only reassurance and support and a minimal amount of physical assistance, and it can be tremendously satisfying and exciting.

Midwives do not look on normal pregnancies and deliveries as ho-hum affairs, even though many doctors seem to be openly bored by them. Doctors often consider normal births to be too time-consuming because they are overworked and overtrained for them. After all, "people who have completed studies of more than 10 years at a university," says Dr. Kloosterman, "are not suited for sitting and watching for hours a natural process taking place as a routine."

Midwives, on the other hand, have *only* the normal to care for and are experts at working with nature. Just as the emergency is more of a challenge to the doctors, the normal is a challenge to us. We want our patients to deliver normally, and we do our best to see that this happens.

"The midwives really enjoy bringing life into the world. They weren't waiting for some wonderful complication to happen. It's obviously a work of love, you can see that."

According to Dr. Kloosterman, "The first task of the midwife is to protect the completely healthy woman against unnecessary interference, impatience, overestimation of technology, and human meddlesomeness. . . . Her second task is to inspire self-confidence and to stimulate the expectant mother in such a way that she considers her reproductive task not a burden but a creative deed accepted by her own free will. . . . Her third task is to be constantly on the watch for abnormalities."

Midwives are not looking for, as one patient put it, "some wonderful complication" to occur so we can demonstrate our skills in an emergency. We are trained to manage the normal pregnancies of healthy women and to conduct normal spontaneous deliveries. We are, in fact, prohibited against using such intervention as general anesthesia, forceps, elective induction, though we are skilled in detecting deviations from the normal and know that we can call in a physician if any occur.

In an era when the cesarean section and forceps rates in many hospitals have reached an unprecedented high, with many doctors preferring to intervene rather than wait to see if the woman progresses normally, ours are comparatively low. Our episiotomy rates are also much lower than those of most traditional doctors. Our need for infant resuscitation is also much less because our mothers—and so the babies—have not been drugged.

We Are a Team with the Doctors: Midwives and physicians work as a team, the doctors acting as back-up in case specialized training and expertise is required. Though we always want a birth to occur spontaneously, there are times when that's just not going to happen. Sometimes there are complications, and the patient will need help in order to deliver a healthy baby. We are so attuned to the progress of a normal pregnancy that it is our responsibility, in our particular hospital, at any rate, to decide when help should be called upon or a consultation is indicated. We are covered by board-certified obstetricians 24 hours a day, seven days a week, and the cooperation of the house staff, the residents, and the attending physicians has been nothing less than great.

In the first two years of our private midwifery service, we accepted 306 patients into our program. Of these, 4.9 percent were transferred out to obstetricians during their pregnancies, and others required the services of a doctor for delivery via forceps or cesarean section. Over 88 percent of the deliveries were normal and spontaneous and were totally managed by the midwives.

Though few of our patients have ever expressed concern that midwives are not doctors, they all want to know what will happen if, in the course of their pregnancies or deliveries, they require medical intervention. Let me explain how this works at our hospital and with most other midwifery services.

"My father's a doctor, and I'm a public-health nurse, but I decided to go to the midwives because I've seen them work, and I know they get much more involved with you."

Because we deal only with what is absolutely normal, we accept only low-risk patients who are in the early part (usually the first three months) of their pregnancies. Each woman is carefully screened, first over the telephone, then through a thorough physical examination and a complete medical history to determine that she is in good physical condition for childbearing. Women, for example, with histories of heart conditions, hypertension, diabetes, kidney disease, severe asthma, epilepsy, etc., as well as those who have had previous cesarean sections would not be considered low risk, and we could not accept them.

We explain to each woman that if any problems that we are not authorized to handle arise during pregnancy or at the time of delivery, she must be transferred out to the care of an obstetrician. A woman with a family history of diabetes is given a glucose tolerance test in her twenty-eighth week of pregnancy; if it proves to be even slightly abnormal, she must be transferred to a doctor. If a patient develops, for example, abnormally high blood pressure or thrombophlebitis (inflammation of a vein), or spills a high concentration of albumin into her urine during pregnancy, we cannot keep her. If she requires medical attention, she is best off in the hands of a doctor who is trained to manage such problems, which concern not only her pregnancy but her general state of health.

Some women progress perfectly normally right up to the point of delivery and then cannot deliver safely without the use of forceps or perhaps a cesarean section. While we do our best to help them bear their babies spontaneously, we must call in the doctors if they can't.

While many complications develop gradually with obvious signals, some problems may be true emergencies. Elevated blood pressure or toxemia, for instance, are detectable as they develop, and we consult with the doctors about the possibility of transferring the patient to medical management. However, hemorrhaging in labor or after delivery always requires medical intervention. In these cases, the best course of treatment is decided by the physician.

Sometimes a woman's membranes have broken but there is no sign of labor within a reasonable length of time (about 12–24 hours), or the labor is very weak. Then the doctors must decide if she needs stimulation or induction, though we may proceed with it. Or a patient is fully dilated and in good labor but, after two hours, is unable to push anymore. This is what we call a prolonged second stage. Then we would consult with the obstetrician to consider forceps or a section.

Babies who decide to arrive as breech presentations (buttocks or feet delivering first) may be delivered vaginally by us if this is deemed to be safe, though in this case we always have an obstetrician scrubbed in the delivery room with us. If the labor does not progress, or there is fetal distress, and a cesarean section or forceps is indicated, the doctor takes over. A doctor also takes over surgically in cases when the baby is too large for the pelvis, or when there is a prolapsed cord—a cord that delivers before the baby's presenting part—a dangerous situation that calls for a cesarean section.

When we deliver twins, we always have a physician, scrubbed, gowned, and gloved, standing by because often an extra pair of hands is needed.

Pediatricians are also called for breech births, cesarean sections, multiple births, and when there are signs of fetal distress.

Nurse-anesthetists attend every delivery and are ready to administer anesthesia if it is needed.

Experienced midwives recognize the earliest signs of any difficulty and know when to call for assistance. We explain every move we make as fully as possible to our patients and let them in on every decision and every question. Though patients are obviously disappointed when they cannot deliver normally as they'd planned, none has ever questioned the final decision. And they know that even when the doctors have to take over, we will stay with them in the delivery room and attend them after the baby is born, an advantage made possible by the location of our midwifery service in a hospital.

WE ARE FLEXIBLE: Nurse-midwives as a group feel that childbirth belongs to the parents, not to the "experts." Just about any way a woman wants to have her baby is agreeable to us. New patients often come to us ready to argue— "I refuse to be shaved, I want the lights dimmed in the delivery room, I don't want to deliver lying down, I don't want any drugs"—and we assure them promptly that they can deliver as they want, within safe limits, of course. While we won't endanger a woman or her baby, we live by very few rules and restrictions.

Our patients have not been the kind of women who walk away from tradition completely. They are the kind of women who question all the routines and traditional procedures and want to know the reasons behind every decision.

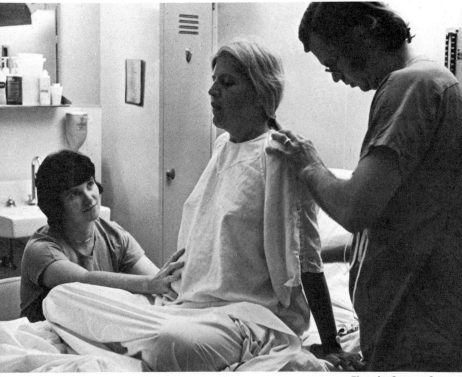

Photo by Suzanne Szasz

Because the midwives' role is not authoritarian but one of friend-adviser, we make a point of sharing everything with our patients. We never do anything *to* them, rather *with* them, explaining our position and our thoughts every step of the way. We are willing to consider any ideas or demands they may have concerning their own childbirth, and we bend to them whenever possible.

> *"On my first visit, I said, 'I don't want any drugs. I don't want to be shaved, and I don't want an enema. An episiotomy is the last thing I'll stand for. What do you say to that?' Barbara said, 'Look, you can have it like you want it. We'll go along with anything you want as long as it's safe for you and the baby.' And they did."*

As Dorothea Lang, one of the country's leading midwives, who has done much to bring about our resurgence, says, "Because we are flexible, nurse-midwives have made many changes in the way childbirth is conducted. Midwives pioneered in many hospitals to allow fathers in the labor and delivery rooms, and they were the first to bring a family orientation to what has been considered a strictly medical event. They have fought for patient's rights, for new birth positions, breast-feeding on the delivery table, rooming-in, and early discharge. Though we do have to abide by some hospital procedures, we have shown that it is quite possible to combine safe childbirth with empathy and compassion."

WE PROVIDE LOW-COST SERVICE: The cost of having a baby today is catastrophic for many families, especially since most medical insurance reimbursements cover very little of it. Some couples cannot pay such costs, and others refuse to, one reason they are increasingly turning to midwifery services, which cost them much less than the services of a private obstetrician combined with skyrocketing hospital rates. Our fees, which include the patient's hospital stay, have become an important added attraction of midwifery.

> *"There's no reason why having a baby has to cost so much. I didn't go to the midwives because they were cheap, but it certainly was a factor to be considered."*

We do not, however, encourage couples to come to us merely because of the lower fees. If they don't believe in midwives and would feel more secure with a physician, then we believe they should spend the extra money to have one. Or they should go to a hospital clinic, many of which provide excellent care and often the chance of a midwife delivery as well, usually at an even lower cost. There has been a marked increase in the number of middle-class women using clinic service in the last few years.

Our fee at Roosevelt Hospital (which approximates midwifery fees elsewhere) was only $459 until March of 1976. At that time, it was increased to $899 to cover the hospital's costs. The fee includes all prenatal visits (once a month at first, then every two weeks, then every week), all laboratory work (blood tests, urinalysis, serology tests, Pap smears, cervical smears, etc.), and prenatal vitamins and iron. It also includes our constant attendance throughout labor, the delivery, plus two days in the hospital with the baby rooming-in as well as circumcision of the male baby if desired. A four-week postpartum examination, which can include family planning (IUD [intra-uterine device], birth-control pills, diaphragm, etc.), is also covered.

There are only two other fees a patient must pay outside of the package price. One is for parent-education classes (in this hospital a six-week series costs $15) and another for the private pediatrician you must engage to examine your baby in the hospital.

If, of course, you must be transferred out of the midwifery program to a doctor because you are no longer considered a low-risk patient, you must then pay him/her an additional fee.

8

The Midwives' Philosophy and Practices

Now, to be more specific, I'm going to explain how the nurse-midwives at Roosevelt Hospital view the "routines" of childbirth procedures. I cannot speak for all midwives everywhere, but I do know a good number of the professionally trained midwives in this country today, and I think just about all of them share my views. We have, after all, been educated the same way: to see childbirth as a natural, normal phenomenon in which our role is to help a woman do her job of having her baby.

Prepared Childbirth: When I first began to practice as a graduate nurse, it was back in the days (not too long ago, either!) when prepared childbirth was new in this country. I admit that I was, like the doctors and other nurses, completely ignorant about it, and when I did hear about it, I was just as skeptical as anyone else in the medical profession. After all, childbirth was a job for professionals. The development of "safe" anesthesias, methods of infant resuscitation, and the acquiescence of women wanting to avoid pain made it a medical procedure to be presided over by experts only. What did a mere woman know about bringing forth a baby?

I'll never forget the first woman who came into the hospital demanding to be allowed to have her baby "naturally." She refused to listen to my advice or that of the residents on duty. (I remember one of them said to her, "Are you out of your mind? You won't be able to take all that pain.") But she sat up in bed, huffing and puffing and blowing, then pushing during the second stage of labor—and did it! She had her baby very calmly without a drop of medication. She proved to me it could be done.

I was astounded and became an immediate convert. I realized that what she was doing, and what other subsequent patients were doing, would help me perform my job of delivering babies naturally and normally when I became a midwife.

I promptly began to study prepared-childbirth methods, which, along with my on-the-job training, made me an ar-

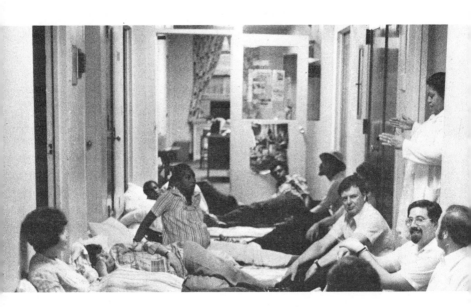

dent advocate. I learned how to work with the women, helping them with their breathing and encouraging them all the way. I even got used to having the father of the baby there with me in the labor room.

And I've seen doctors change right before my eyes, too, doctors who were taught *by their patients* that women who actively participated in their childbirth, who were unafraid and more attuned to what was happening to them, were able to have babies more easily. And that the babies came out in much better condition as well.

> *"I was looking for someone who was really interested in natural childbirth. It's not always easy to tell if a doctor is enthusiastic about it because it's something they have to agree to today even if they don't wholeheartedly like it. But there was no doubt that midwives are enthusiastic because their practice depends on it."*

Today, all of our private midwifery patients at this hospital are required to take some kind of prepared-childbirth education. Because the hospital conducts classes within its own facility, even a good number of clinic patients attend the courses. But the women are free to take classes anywhere they choose. The midwives do not advocate any particular method, and we are familiar with them all. I have found that any method works so long as the woman believes in it.

It's been estimated that up to one-half of the pregnant women in America today attend parent-education classes. There are classes in every major city in the country, most of them in the hospitals. You can find out where classes are given in your community by calling the hospitals, asking your midwife or doctor, or by writing to the Maternity Center Association, 48 East 92nd Street, New York, N. Y. 10028; the International Childbirth Education Association, Inc., P.O. Box 5852, Milwaukee, Wisconsin 53220; or ASPO, the American Society of Psycho-Prophylaxis in Obstetrics, 1523 L Street, N.W., Washington, D.C. 20005.

Just as it did in my case, the demand for the new child-birth has usually come from patients. Because women became insistent that the physician or hospital go along with their demands or they would find others who would, the medical profession has radically changed its attitudes, though only in the last five years or so. And while some obstetricians and institutions remain rigid in their adherence to their traditional ways, I think most now go along, at least to some extent, with prepared childbirth. A woman who is determined to have her baby the new way should make *certain* her doctor (if she can't find a midwifery service) and the hospital not only go along but are enthusiastic about it.

The concept of preparation began with an English obstetrician, Dr. Grantly Dick-Read, who wrote a book called *Childbirth Without Fear*, which was published in 1932 but only became popular much later. Based on the now-proven premise that fear causes tension, and tension intensifies pain, he attempted to reduce fear through education and exercise. The idea began to take root in the U.S. in the 1950s.

Later, a French physician, Dr. Fernand Lamaze, introduced a more advanced approach called the psychoprophylactic method. This method, which also emphasized knowledge of the physiology and psychology of childbirth, set forth a group of prescribed breathing techniques to be practiced by the woman during her contractions. The Lamaze method was popularized here by Marjorie Karmel's book, *Thank You, Dr. Lamaze*, published in 1959.

These new and revolutionary ideas, which stemmed from Europe, were first investigated and propagated not by the medical profession in this country but by lay groups, notably the Maternity Center Association, and later, the International Childbirth Education Association. Because these groups initiated the earliest maternal-education programs in the U.S., they were in touch with parent organizations that were springing up here and there throughout the nation and realized from the questions they were being asked that women were anxious to know more, to participate more, and to have much more of a voice in what was happening to them.

The educational groups promptly found that they had the support of nurse-midwives because of our concept of childbirth as a normal, natural event, and many of us joined them in promoting parent education. They, on the other hand, gained our knowledge about the possibilities of women's abilities to participate in their own childbirths.

While, from my experience, the Lamaze approach is the most widely used today along with a modified Lamaze technique, other methods are growing in popularity, notably the most recent Bradley method, which stresses muscle relaxation, not disciplined breathing. Both Lamaze and Bradley require that the father, some other close friend or relative, or a trained companion remain with the mother throughout labor and delivery to coach and encourage her.

All of this introduction leads up to my main point: Midwives are natural allies of prepared childbirth. Because we want to deliver babies spontaneously to mothers who are awake and working right along with us, we insist that our private patients learn *some* prepared childbirth method and that they attend classes regularly. We know the methods very well, and we are capable not only of coaching our mothers but of giving on-the-job training if it becomes apparent that they haven't grasped the techniques well enough. (In fact, many nurse-midwives teach parent-education classes.)

> *"We were both so nervous when we got to the labor room that I forgot how to do the breathing exercises, and my husband couldn't help at first. But the midwife started us off, and we carried on beautifully after that."*

A woman who has attended parent-education classes learns what is happening within her body throughout her pregnancy, gets a chance to ask questions and find out everything she wants to know. She knows what to expect when she goes into labor, what each stage signifies, and how to deal with it. When I say to her, for example, "You're seven centimeters dilated, and the baby's head is at 0 station," she understands that she's about to reach transition, which is the end of the first stage of labor, and she isn't mystified about what's coming next.

> *"No matter how you do it, it's hard work. You might as well be in charge of yourself."*

Because she knows, her fear evaporates. When fear is eliminated, pain not only becomes more bearable but is actually lessened. Some women say to me, in fact, that what they feel isn't really pain at all, merely discomfort or pressure. Others definitely feel it as pain but know—from their training—just how strong it will be, how long it will last, and that there's time between contractions to relax and pre-

Photo by Suzanne Szasz

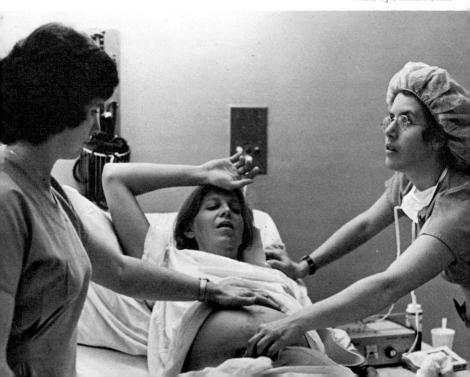

pare for the next one. They know the discomfort will stop and they'll have a break. Women uneducated about childbirth often feel that labor is like one continual, never-ending contraction that soon becomes terrifying and overwhelming. Fear is what prevents them from assuming control and panics them into putting themselves totally into the hands of the "experts."

> *"The last time, I was in that labor room all alone, with someone coming in to check once in a while. My husband was waiting downstairs. I was terrified. The doctor arrived at the last minute to deliver the baby. This time, Barbara—and my husband—were with me from the moment I went into the labor room until we celebrated after it was all over. The whole thing was a thrill."*

The intense concentration of a laboring woman on the breathing or relaxation techniques she's learned helps reduce tension and therefore pain and also distracts her, making her less aware of her discomfort. It gives her something to focus on beside her discomfort. Not only that, but she's in control. She is working *with* her contractions, not against them. This helps the uterus to relax and the cervix to dilate more readily, so the birth moves along more rapidly.

The idea of prepared childbirth is not to ensure that a woman will make it without medication but to help her participate as much as she can in the birth. But women who come prepared, I have found, need medication much less frequently than those who haven't. In fact, the unprepared mothers almost always require some. I'm not saying that we don't ever give our patients some mild medication to take the edge off their discomfort, but not nearly as often or as much. As Elizabeth Bing, a well-known Lamaze teacher, says, "There's really never a question of 'making it.' After all, when you end up with a baby, no one is going to give you a C minus!"

Studies have shown—and I can bear them out—that

mothers who actively participate in their childbirth tend to
have significantly shorter labors as well as less medication.
They require less obstetric intervention (heavily drugged
women can't always cooperate in pushing the baby out and
must often be delivered by forceps) and are much happier
with their accomplishment when it is over.

> *"Having a baby is never a picnic, at least for me. It hurts.
> But with the midwife it was not a nightmare. Actually, it was
> very exciting, and I felt I'd really accomplished something
> truly special."*

Midwives are happier, too. We have to have the active
participation of the woman if we're going to deliver her
baby the "new" way—normally and spontaneously. This is
a partnership we've formed together. It's like a symphony.
She, with the father's help, plays all the instruments, while
we conduct and manage, encourage and support, and make
sure the music comes out the way it's supposed to—coordinated, smooth, on time, and beautiful.

FATHERS AS PART OF THE FAMILY: At Roosevelt Hospital,
and at most hospitals in which midwives practice, the father of the baby (or another chosen person) is encouraged to
stay with the patient from the moment she comes into the
hospital till after the baby is born and she is back in her
room. After that, the father has unlimited visiting privileges
from eight in the morning till eight at night. He can hold
his baby as much as he wants, and instead of being made to
feel like an unwanted intruder, he is actively encouraged to
establish an immediate relationship with his baby.

> *"This was definitely not going to be a lonely business. I
> wanted my man right there with me the whole time. After all,
> it's his baby, too."*

About half of the hospitals in the U.S. now permit fathers
into the labor room, though many refuse them entry to the

delivery room. Often the obstetrician is the one who bars fathers from either place; many obstetricians still object to their presence. I've talked to some doctors who feel this way and discovered that they find fathers distracting and inhibiting. "Listen," one doctor said to me some time ago, "I want to do my job without some guy constantly asking me questions and getting in my way." Another felt that childbirth isn't always pretty to watch, that the father might faint or get sick. "I don't think a lot of men want to be there, anyway—it's the women who insist they stay."

The truth is that young couples today are insisting that they go through this momentous experience together, and they are finding doctors or midwives and hospitals who allow them to do it. I am happy to say that the obstetricians at Roosevelt Hospital encourage fathers to be actively involved with the birth of their children. Midwives have always been family-oriented. We feel that the father will not only help the woman immeasurably, both emotionally and

Photo by Suzanne Szasz

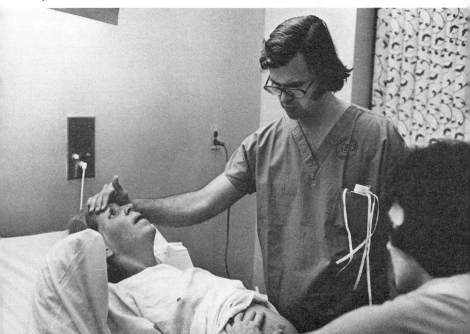

physically, but will feel a closer bond with her and their baby when it's over.

Childbirth is no time for a woman to be torn from the arms of the person closest to her; it's no time to be alone and afraid, isolated in a strange and sterile place and tended (not too tenderly sometimes) by strangers. That's why mid-wives always stay with their patients constantly from the time they start active labor, and that's why we want the fa-thers there. We don't leave fathers to pace anxiously up and down in an unfamiliar waiting room while the women go through this experience without them. Of course, some men don't want to take part in this event—and we respect those wishes, too—but nine times out of ten, they do.

> *"My husband didn't think he wanted to stay around for the whole thing. He thought he'd find it too upsetting and he'd only mess me up emotionally. But he really got excited and in-volved, and he says he wouldn't have missed it for anything."*

The fathers of the babies we midwives deliver at Roose-velt are invited to come along on any or all prenatal visits. We've found it's particularly useful if they come to the first visit, when the women meet us for the first time. We never ask them to leave the room even when we do internal exam-inations, and we always encourage them to ask us any questions they may have.

Not only the fathers but the siblings of our babies-to-be may come for the prenatal visits. A lot of them do and get great delight listening to the fetal heartbeat through our fetoscopes. Because we realize this is truly a family affair—what could be more of one?—we want them to feel part of it.

The fathers are very helpful in the labor room. They're not spectators but active participants. We put them right to work. They've been trained in the parent-education classes how to coach the women with their breathing exercises or to remind them how to relax their muscles. Because they've been educated also, they understand the stages of labor and can follow the sequence of events. They feel free to ask questions and take part in making any decisions (we make a point of explaining and discussing everything we do) because midwives and parents are, by this time, an extended family. We're comfortable with each other. We call each other by our first names (from the first prenatal visit), so we don't come across as "authority figures" whose every utterance is hallowed and indisputable.

However, we have expertise in managing pregnancies and deliveries; families look to us as professionals for support and encouragement.

> *Husband: "I'm naturally squeamish, but this seemed like a natural part of life. It was natural, and it was my baby. I felt I worked with the midwife like a team, almost as if we were partners. I did most of the coaching until the pushing stage; then the midwife assisted more because my wife wanted her to help as well."*

The support person who accompanies our patients knows how to massage away tension, apply pressure to their backs, or support a leg (we support the other) when they reach the pushing stage. If they don't know how to perform any of these duties, we are there to show them.

If a fetal monitor—which records the fetal heartbeat and uterine contractions—is used, the parents quickly learn when a contraction is coming. This allows the patient to start her breathing early and not be taken by surprise by the sensation.

Most important of all, the father provides emotional support. A woman who is going through a strenuous, trying, and sometimes very uncomfortable experience needs love and concern from someone who truly cares for her.

A father can help in the delivery room, too, supporting the woman's back while she pushes, wiping her forehead, holding her hand. His presence there with her as they watch the baby emerge from the birth canal gives them both immeasurable joy. Many of our fathers take pictures of the birth, and that's just fine with us as long as they don't use flash. I always ask them to save a couple of exposures for me to photograph the three of them together.

> Husband: *"In some hospitals, when you have natural child-birth, the full responsibility is on the father for commanding the mother. I wanted to be there, and I wanted to help, but I didn't want to be in charge. I don't think I could have handled that too well."*

And afterward, while the baby is resting in his mother's arms, we celebrate with congratulations all around and maybe even a juice toast.

ATTENDANCE IN THE LABOR ROOM: We never leave our patients alone in the labor room. We make a pact with them

Photo by Suzanne Szasz

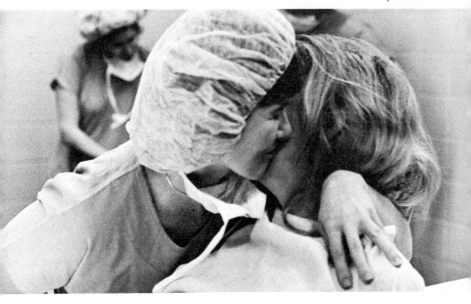

and give them our guarantee that we will come into the hospital when they do and stay there with them—no matter how many hours it might take—until they've delivered.

"My friend was all alone in the labor room for six hours except for the nurse and a resident once in a while. I'm terrified of being alone then."

We never go out to lunch or down the hall to read a magazine, to the operating room for emergency surgery, or to the office to see other patients while they carry on alone. If we must be out of the room for a short while, one of the other midwives relieves us. A vital part of our role is to be with our patients constantly.

Being in labor, especially the first time around, and in a strange place, can be frightening even if a patient has had prepared-childbirth training and all the reassurances we can give her. Sometimes she, and often her husband, are uncer-

Photo by Richard Martin

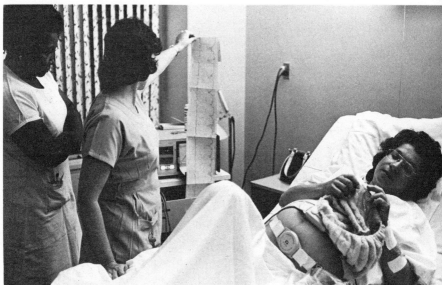

tain about what's going to happen and how they're going to cope. That we're there with them gives them tremendous emotional support and eliminates more fear and tension, and therefore pain, than the best sedative yet discovered.

> *"I knew she wouldn't be out playing tennis when it was time for me to get into the hospital."*

There is usually little for us to do during the early stages of labor, especially if the father or a friend is there to coach, except to encourage, reassure, and refresh the father or patient in breathing techniques or massage. At this time we can also explain how the fetal monitor works. We show them how to assist mother nature while we offer comfort and support. Our presence in that room is invaluable, and many women feel it was their most important reason for seeking us out to begin with.

In the later stages of labor, our expertise in childbirth—judging whether everything is within normal bounds, suggesting medication if the patient needs it, helping with the breathing and then with the pushing, knowing just what is happening when—is even more helpful.

Though many obstetricians would love to be able to spend so much time and attention on their patients, they usually have busy schedules that won't allow it. So what usually happens is that a doctor gets a call from his patient who is going into labor just when his office is filled with other patients or he has a woman ready for surgery. So he says, "Check into the hospital and I'll be there just as soon as I can." Often he arrives just before the baby comes, and the patient has been left in the hands, sympathetic but rushed, of the nurses.

Midwives, who don't have to be concerned with emergency surgery and gynecologic patients, are able to be there in the hospital, in the labor room, from start to finish. They not only provide support, guidance, and medical knowledge but can also act as the patient's advocate. After all, she is not always in a position to bargain in the labor room.

SHAVING OR PREPPING: Shaving the pubic hair is still routinely done in most hospitals, but it is not done to our midwifery patients because we feel that it is an annoyance and an indignity. We don't feel a prep is necessary. The reasons given for shaving are that the pubic hair harbors bacteria and that it gets in the way of an episiotomy if one is needed. In fact, removing the hair does not reduce the incidence of infection, and if any hair gets in our way while we're delivering the baby or repairing an episiotomy, we merely push it aside or perhaps clip it a little with scissors.

> Husband: "We had a one-hour talk with the obstetrician, and we pinned him down, made him tell us where he stood. We found out he always did episiotomies, always shaved, always started the intravenous drip. Besides that, the hospital didn't have rooming-in and was not much in favor of breast-feeding. We came to the decision to leave him and look elsewhere."

ENEMAS: We do not routinely give our patients an enema when they go into labor. (Actually, we don't routinely do anything!) To us, there's an individual decision to be made for each person. Usually, we feel an enema is unnecessary, and there is no need to subject a patient to any unpleasant procedure for the sake of conformity or because that's what has always been done.

But sometimes we do recommend enemas: It may be easier for a woman to push if her colon is evacuated. And sometimes a woman will come into the hospital constipated, especially if she's been taking iron. It is part of our policy always to explain all of our reasoning to our patients so they know exactly why we think this or any other procedure will help in their particular case.

MEDICATION: A midwife's job is to deliver babies normally and spontaneously. Deliveries of babies to heavily drugged, perhaps unconscious mothers who are unable to participate in the birth are not considered normal and spontaneous and are not part of our repertoire.

> *"She used her judgment and waited till she felt I really needed a little medication. Then she gave me just enough to make me relax between contractions."*

On the other hand, we do not believe in denying a mild tranquilizer or pain reliever to a woman who feels she needs it. Our purpose is not to make certain that every patient can "make it all the way" without any help at all, and we do administer a minimal amount of medication if our patients request it. Childbirth can be quite uncomfortable, and sometimes a relaxant is needed to help them manage. Eighty percent of our private patients, however, have no

Photo by Suzanne Szasz

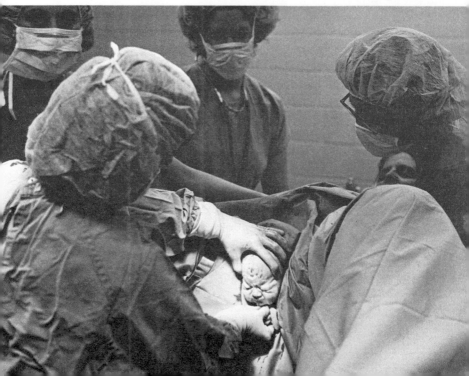

medication at all or are only minimally medicated. None of them are ever drugged, and their babies do not arrive limp and sluggish because of overmedication and so do not need resuscitation as many other babies do.

Our Apgar scoring (a numerical measurement of the baby's condition at birth) is proof of that. At one minute after delivery, 96.8 percent of our babies have scored 8 or better (of a possible 10), which is excellent. At five minutes, 99.2 percent have had an Apgar score of 8 or better.

Not too many years ago, many patients were heavily sedated, so thoroughly that they did not feel—or remember—a bit of pain. They were often given scopolamine, a drug that doesn't relieve pain but blots out the memory of it. Today, the trend, especially in the larger cities and major medical centers, is toward less medication, though it is still routinely used by many practitioners to one degree or another. Still quite popular these days are regional block anesthesias, which numb the lower part of a woman's body so that she feels nothing. The disadvantage may be that she may need a forceps delivery because she cannot push sufficiently.

Occasionally, you will still find doctors who give general anesthesia to their laboring patients, who then cannot take part. Overmedicating with narcotics or barbituates can prolong labor, depress fetal respiration and heartbeat, and can affect the baby's central nervous system, at least temporarily. Overmedicated babies may have a much harder time responding to their environments. They are less alert and less active.

Our patients, because of the parent-education classes they attend and our reassurance and emotional support, do not come to the labor room panic-stricken and ignorant. The fear and tension that have been proved to heighten discomfort in childbirth have been largely eliminated, and so most of the women do not want or need much medication.

Every labor, of course, is different, and every woman

reacts in her own way. Many women find they can easily, especially if their labor moves along quickly, get by with no medication at all. Others do much better with a minimal amount so that they can cope with the contractions, relax between them, and keep themselves together and composed. Some patients come into the hospital quite rigid in their disdain for medication, though parent-education teachers no longer press them to reject it under every circumstance, as many of them did in the early days of prepared childbirth. We midwives do not insist that a woman accept medication; in fact, we encourage her to carry on as long as possible without it. But sometimes we feel it would be a good idea for her to accept a very light, quite minimal, amount of a pain reliever or tranquilizer to help her relax. We reassure her that she has not failed a "test" if she needs the medication.

> *"I didn't want to take any drugs because I know they're bad for the baby, but I wasn't sure I'd make it without them. But I did. The midwife encourages you and helps you, and so does your husband, and you find you can do it."*

As with everything else, our decision to offer medication is individualized, and it is each patient's prerogative to accept or reject it. We consider her needs and desires and the point of labor she has reached. Never do we give enough medication to adversely affect the baby, nor to cause the mother to fall asleep between contractions so that she panics when she is suddenly gripped by a contraction without time to prepare herself. She must always remain in control and on top of them so that she may continue to do her job of bringing forth her baby.

EPISIOTOMIES: I'd estimate that 95 percent of our patients tell us, usually during their first prenatal visit or even on the telephone when they are making their initial appointment, that they definitely do not want to have an episiotomy. We tell them we will do our very best to avoid one, but that this is a decision that *must* be made at the time of the delivery.

An episiotomy is a surgical cut made below the vagina, enlarging the vaginal opening for the baby's head. It is done in order to prevent the perineal tissues from tearing. We prefer to deliver over intact perineums (the external surface between the vagina and the anus) if that is possible and safe for the baby and the mother.

To do this successfully is often quite a challenge; it is not always easy, and it requires extra time and patience—ours and the patient's. If the midwife and the woman can cooperate closely so that her pushing is in perfect control, and if the midwife can make sure the baby's head is delivering slowly and properly, and the tissue has a chance to stretch gradually—sometimes helped along with massage—there is a good possibility that an episiotomy won't be needed.

If, however, the tissue hasn't had a chance to stretch, or if the baby's head is particularly large for the opening, or

Photo by Suzanne Szasz

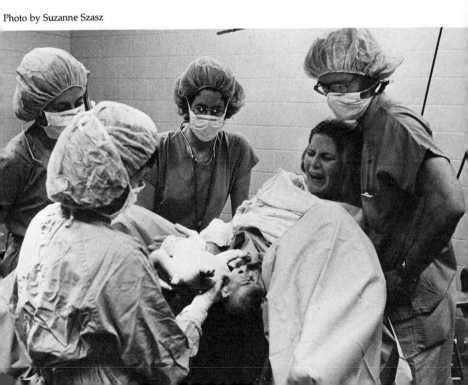

there's a need for a speedy delivery (usually when there are signs of fetal distress), or a laceration seems imminent, then midwives would make the cut to prevent the tear. A tear can go in any direction to any degree and is much more difficult to repair than a clean incision. Before we make the cut, we inject a local anesthetic into the surrounding tissues. This does not affect the mother's ability to push. We do not need much because the pressure of the baby's head on the perineum creates its own natural numbing of the nerves.

> *"I had to have an episiotomy because the baby's head was really large, but she explained why she had to do it, and it was logical, so I didn't really mind."*

Women often object to an episiotomy because they feel it isn't "natural," or because they want to avoid the discomfort of the stitches and the healing afterward. Sometimes they object because they think it is a procedure perfected and pushed by male physicians so that the vagina will be tightened for the benefit of male sexual pleasure later. But we always explain, at the time, exactly why we think the incision should be made, if indeed we do think so, and by looking in the overhead mirror above the delivery table, the patient can see for herself just how tightly the tissues are stretching. I have never had a woman object to the procedure when she has understood why I thought it was needed.

Frankly, I enjoy delivering a baby without cutting. It's an accomplishment for both of us. For that reason and because we always want to give every patient what she wants if we can, my goal is to avoid the episiotomy if it will be safe.

INDUCTIONS: Midwives *never* induce labor for our own convenience or for our patients', either, for that matter. Inductions have become rather a scandal in this country because some obstetricians are so busy that they like to be able to schedule their deliveries at times that are convenient for them. Sometimes doctors induce babies because they're going away on vacation or have busy schedules. And sometimes mothers have asked to be induced because they have vacation plans, their husbands are going on a business trip, or they want an additional tax deduction before the end of the year! But midwives will *never* consent to elective inductions.

Induction is the artificial stimulation of labor by the use of oxytocins (natural or chemical hormones). The reasons we do not use it when it is not medically indicated are that, first of all, an induced labor may not be normal and spontaneous, and it may not always be totally safe. Often, with artificial stimulation that is not very carefully controlled and constantly watched, the contractions become too strong and too close together, and not only does the mother have a much harder time coping with them, but there could be problems for both mother and baby.

> *"My first baby was induced, and it was an awful experience because the pains were so intense and so concentrated that I couldn't pull myself together at all. Besides, I didn't know how to do those breathing exercises. It was an experience I'd rather forget. This time I coped through the whole thing with only a tiny amount of medication."*

There are times, however, when induction or stimulation of labor is necessary for the safety of mother and baby, and at those times midwives, at least in our hospital, may decide, after consultation with the obstetrician in charge, that it is the best route.

If it is determined—through testing of the amniotic fluid (fluid surrounding the fetus in utero)—that a mature baby is at least three weeks overdue, and there is no sign of labor, then it is usually decided that it would be wiser to deliver the baby than to wait any longer.

If the mother has a medical problem such as diabetes or toxemia, sometimes the physicians decide to induce labor, but this is not a normal situation, so it would not be managed by midwives.

If a woman's membranes have ruptured, and labor does not begin so that she will deliver within a reasonable amount of time (we consider that to be within 12–24 hours), or if the labor is very weak, and we know the baby is at term, we consult with a physician about whether some stimulation is needed. Because of the increased possibility of amnionitis (infection of the amniotic sac) once the membranes have ruptured, it is usually considered safer to start labor.

Before any stimulation is begun, x-rays of the pelvis must be made of any woman having her first child to be certain the bony structure is large enough to accommodate the baby's head. With the woman who has had previous babies, x-rays are usually not necessary if the baby is not overly large.

When we come to the conclusion, together with the doctors, that stimulation is indicated, we discuss the situation with the couple, tell them our findings, and explain the procedure.

Our inductions are made with intravenous infusions of pitocin, a form of oxytocin, and are very carefully monitored so that the contractions start very slowly and gradually build in intensity, as with normal labor, and never become too strong or too frequent, again like normal labor. When we stimulate, it is important to use the fetal monitor machine so that we have a very clear picture of the contractions we are getting. The amount of pitocin the woman is receiving can and must be carefully and constantly adjusted if her labor is to imitate nature.

When a patient asks me during her prenatal visits if we ever induce labor, I explain all these possibilities to her and let her know that we never choose induction unless it is definitely indicated for her and the baby's safety. *Never* do we do it for convenience.

GETTING OUT OF BED: Most hospitals and most doctors in this country discourage laboring patients from getting up out of bed, maintaining that it isn't safe. Midwives do not feel this way. Our patients at this hospital are asked to telephone us from home when labor begins, to keep us informed about their progress, and to come into the hospital only when their labor is truly under way—or their membranes have ruptured. In the meantime, we encourage them to be as active as they feel like being—go for a walk, watch television, or cook; there's no need to stay in bed.

Once the patient arrives at the hospital and goes to the labor room, she usually isn't very anxious to get up and walk around. But if she does want to move around, that's perfectly fine with us. It will not only make her comfortable but can actually speed up labor by relaxing and distracting her and helping to position the baby's head in the birth canal. The only exception to this is when the membranes have ruptured. Then we are concerned about the possibility of a prolapsed cord as well as infection, and so we prefer the patient with ruptured membranes to stay in bed. But she certainly may sit up or assume any position she finds comfortable.

MONITORING: The use of the recently developed fetal heart monitor has been hotly debated. Many women strongly object to being "hooked up to a machine," which they feel dehumanizes them and keeps them needlessly confined. Others, having read about the monitors, want to be certain we have them on hand. The fetal monitor beeps out a continuous reading of the fetal heartbeat and lets us know if the rhythm is abnormal or if there is any sign of fetal distress. Heartbeat, of course, can be monitored by a hand-held instrument called a Doppler or by a fetoscope, although these methods are not nearly as accurate.

The monitor also provides a graph of both the heartbeat and the contractions the patient is having. With this, we have a record of just how steady the beat is, how strong the contractions are, and whether there are any significant changes.

Monitors are attached externally or internally. The external monitor is a belt that goes around the mother's abdomen. The internal monitor consists of electrodes that are passed up the vagina and through the cervix and attached to the presenting part, usually the scalp, of the baby. Of course, this means the membranes must already have ruptured. The internal monitor is much more sensitive and revealing than the external and is used when we think there is any real risk that the fetus is in trouble or when we can't get enough information externally.

> *"It was very helpful to be told when the contractions were coming so I could get ready. It was very tiring, and I found it much more painful than I ever expected, but she worked with me, encouraged me, and it was absolutely essential for me psychologically. She and Michael kept it up for three or four hours, and they got me through it. I did have a little sedative, but I was awake for the whole thing and watched the baby come out. I couldn't have done it without her."*

When we first introduced monitors, just at the time our private practice was begun, I anticipated an overwhelmingly negative response from our patients. After all, it would require belts around their middles and being plugged into a machine, and our women, we knew, wanted everything to be as natural as possible. To my surprise, I found that most of our patients, being the kind of women who want to know what's going on all the time, *wanted* to try them. The more these women know, the more they want to know. We offered the monitors, explaining that they were perfectly free to accept or refuse, but that we felt the monitors could be most helpful in some cases. Personally, I feel the monitors are extremely helpful. With their ability to plot a woman's labor and the baby's heartbeat in a continuous pattern, they pick up much more and better information than even a very experienced midwife or doctor could acquire by feeling with her hand or hearing with her ears.

I encourage the monitor when there is the possibility of the need to stimulate labor, when we find meconium (stool) in the amniotic fluid, which may signify fetal distress, or when, for any reason, we think we really need to know more about heartbeat and/or contractions.

If we use the external monitor and find labor is perfectly normal, then we can always take it off. If the patient wants to get up and walk around or go to the bathroom (if her membranes are intact), the monitor may easily be removed.

Since we have been using the monitors, we have found our patients to be astonishingly enthusiastic about them. The normal readings make them feel safe, and besides, they are able to tell—before they can actually feel it—when a contraction is beginning. They can start their breathing or relaxing exercises early and get a good start on their control of the discomfort. We have found that fathers, in their desire to be helpful, usually love to be the ones to take over the job of alerting the women to the impending contractions.

INTRAVENOUS INFUSIONS: Usually, when a woman gives birth in an American hospital, a vein in her arm is routinely opened and an intravenous tube inserted sometime during her labor. This is done "just in case." Just in case she becomes dehydrated, or will need stimulation for her contractions, or relief from pain, if she's in any danger of hemorrhaging after the delivery, or may require a cesarean section and therefore anesthesia, or perhaps will need a blood transfusion. The feeling of most midwives is that if all is going normally, she will probably not need any infusions and so needn't be bothered by the tube, which tends to be uncomfortable and keeps her confined to her bed.

If, of course, the patient is dehydrated or needs medication or stimulation, or we anticipate any problems—this is a situation in which everything is not going to go perfectly smoothly 100 percent of the time—then we start the intravenous. It takes just a few seconds. The only time during a normal delivery that we might start an intravenous automatically is when the patient has had many previous babies. The more babies, the more the uterus relaxes, and the more chance of postpartum bleeding, which can often be controlled by intravenous infusions of oxytocins.

THE BIRTH POSITION: Because we know that gravity will help push the baby down, that lying flat can produce unnecessary stress on the circulatory system, midwives make a practice of propping their patients up into a semisitting position with stiff pillows or a birth wedge behind their backs. This way, the patient can push more comfortably and also actually see what is happening at the other end of the delivery table. And when she is pushing, her support person—usually the father of the baby—supports her in an even higher position.

Some of the newer maternity hospitals do have either

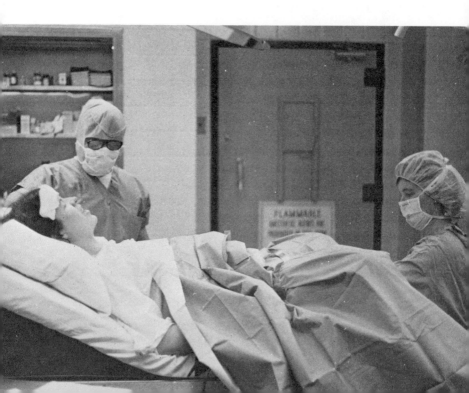

special beds with back supports, or wedges, which allow a woman to deliver in a more upright position if she finds that more comfortable.

Most of the time, we do use stirrups, but keep them as close together as possible, much closer than the accepted standard distance as well as lower because it's more comfortable for the patient and helps us avoid episiotomies, as the perineum isn't so widely stretched. Some patients have objected to the stirrups, and in those cases we haven't used them. Though stirrups make it more convenient for us, we want to be as flexible as possible and do whatever our patient wants if we can do it safely.

We've been asked if we ever strap our women down. The answer is: *never.* They are never so heavily drugged that they become disoriented and out of touch enough to need such treatment. Besides, strapping is the last indignity.

DELIVERING IN BED: At the present time it is our hospital policy to have women deliver not in the labor bed, but on the table in the delivery room so that emergency equipment is immediately available if we should happen to need it. A few of the newest maternity centers have labor beds that easily convert to delivery tables so there's no need to move from bed to table, a procedure many women find very annoying when they're most uncomfortable in the last stages of labor. Eventually, I think all hospitals will have these.

DIMMING THE LIGHTS: Most of the women who come to us, being avid readers of everything concerning childbirth, have read *Birth Without Violence,* a book written by a French physician, Dr. Frederick Leboyer, and want to know if we endorse his suggestions for nontraumatic births.

Actually, midwives were following many of his recommendations long before we had ever heard of him. We keep the delivery room quiet and calm, we do not spank the baby on his bottom, we delay cutting the cord until it stops pulsating, we lay the baby on his mother's abdomen as soon as we see that all is going well, and we give the infant to his mother to hold and nurse, if she wishes, as soon as the cord is cut.

> *"After the cord stopped pulsating and was cut, she gave me the baby to hold in my arms. Afterward, I saw the placenta and she explained where it was attached to me and to the baby."*

Though dimming the lights in the delivery room immediately after the birth was not one of our previous practices, we are perfectly happy to do so if our patients request it—but only after we know whether the baby is pink and in good condition, which we can't determine in the dark. Once the baby's satisfactory condition has been established, if we need light to repair an episiotomy or deliver the placenta, we can use a small spotlight aimed directly at the perineum while the rest of the room is darkened.

> *"I'd read that having the delivery room quiet and dark was best for the baby. It wouldn't be so traumatic for him. When I mentioned that to the midwife, she said, 'Why not?' If that's the way you want it, I'll just use a little spotlight after I see the baby is in good shape. And I won't let anyone make a sound above a whisper.'"*

CUTTING THE CORD: Midwives do not believe in clamping the umbilical cord just as soon as the baby is born, though that is the tradition in this country. We deliver the baby, wipe off its face, and suck out the mucus in its mouth, carefully checking the general appearance of the newborn. Only when the cord stops pulsating—meaning that there is no more circulation of blood between mother and baby—do we clamp the cord. That additional 60 cc. of blood in the cord belongs to the baby, and we want the baby to have it.

Not only is delayed clamping good for the baby, but it's good for the mother, too, as the continued circulation shortens the third stage of labor—the separation and delivery of the placenta.

"She gave me the baby right on the table, and I nursed her. I felt very safe, very warm."

There are times when we must clamp the cord quickly, however, in the rare instances when the baby is having some difficulty, when it needs resuscitation with oxygen or an unusual amount of suction.

Many of our mothers want to hold their babies immediately after birth. We're all for that and once the cord stops pulsating and is cut, we wrap the baby in a sterile blanket and give it to her or the father to hold.

EARLY DISCHARGE: Our package price at Roosevelt includes two days in the hospital, the patient going home on the morning of the third day. We find that most of our patients want to go home quickly; they're healthy young women who haven't been heavily medicated, are up out of bed right after delivery, usually feel just fine, and want to get home and get on with their lives. They do not love hospitals, and they want to leave in the shortest period of time that's safe.

If a woman doesn't feel ready to leave so soon, she is certainly welcome to stay another day or two. And, occasionally, the attending pediatrician may decide it would be a good idea if the baby stays an extra day or two just to be certain all is well.

Most midwifery programs do allow for early discharge, and many obstetricians are following this trend as well.

ROOMING-IN: Because hospitals that employ midwives are almost always the most avant-garde in their approach to

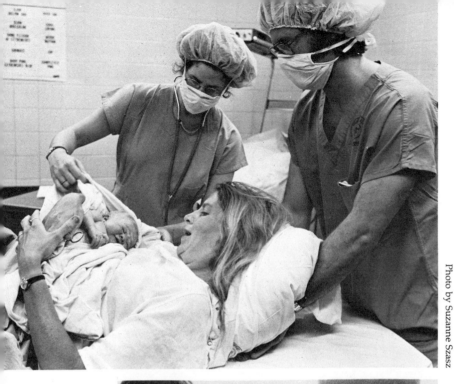

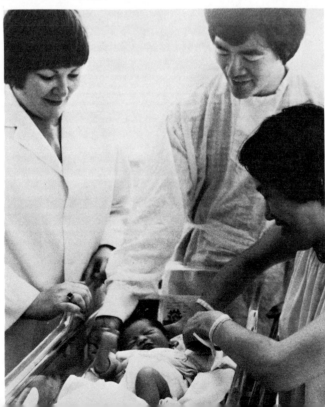

childbirth, most of them have a rooming-in policy. This means that the newborn babies remain with their mothers in their rooms for their entire hospital stay. In our hospital, the babies of our patients stay right there in the delivery room with their parents for perhaps a half hour or more after birth, getting to know each other. If the mothers want to nurse, they are encouraged to do it. If the fathers want to hold their infants, we are delighted. Then the newborns are taken to the nursery for examination and stabilization of temperature and returned promptly to the mothers' room, where they stay day and night until they leave the hospital.

Rooming-in was standard in hospitals in the U.S. until the turn of the century, and of course the great majority of mothers gave birth at home. After that, nurseries became the norm. (The idea was to prevent the spread of infection.) Here the babies remained, presided over by nurses except for a brief glimpse after birth and prescribed visits to their mothers at certain feeding times, starting many hours later.

Now the trend has turned back to rooming-in, spurred by studies, especially one made by two pediatricians, Drs. Marshall Klaus and John Kennell, at Case Western Reserve Medical School in Cleveland, which have shown that mothers and newborns develop a much closer emotional relationship if they are allowed to be together during the first hours and days of life. This period of time, what the two doctors call a "maternal sensitive period," is an important bonding period, a time when a close attachment, emotionally and physically, is formed.

Studies show that without it normal maternal nurturing responses are demonstrably inhibited and sometimes never completely recovered. A woman who is separated from her new baby finds her feelings about the child may even include resentment and a sense of intrusion. And the baby's psychological development and his future relationship with his parents may be vitally affected.

Mothers whose babies room in become much more comfortable with them in a practical sense as well because they have a chance to get used to their tiny bodies, their little noises and movements. They feed them, feel them, care for them, and sleep alongside them in a reassuring setting in which they can ask questions and get help with anything from diapering to breast-feeding. In our hospital, the midwives as well as the nurses and the infant-care technicians are there for support.

The babies stay with their mothers 24 hours a day (unless the patient prefers it otherwise; some like "modified" rooming-in which means the baby goes to the nursery for the night). If you are interested in rooming-in, be sure to check this out thoroughly before you enter the hospital.

A bonding period is almost as important for the father, too. The father should be present, if he wishes, during labor and delivery, and he should be allowed to hold his baby as much as he wants in the first few days after birth. Otherwise, he, too, may feel alienated. One father said to me, "My feeling about this baby is so different from my feelings at first about our other one. It's like she's much more mine because I've been so involved with her. Last time, I was kept waiting downstairs while she was born, and then I could only see her through the glass wall. I was a stranger."

With rooming-in, the father is permitted to visit mother and baby at any time during the day and to stay as long as he likes. Other visitors must wait for the regular visiting hours.

9

A Patient's Progress

Though I have explained throughout this book how we run our particular private midwifery service, I am going to give you a step-by-step outline so that, if you choose a midwifery-managed childbirth, you will have a realistic idea of what to expect.

INITIAL CONTACT: Our first contact with a new patient is a telephone conversation when she calls to inquire about our program and to ask if we might accept her. We take a brief medical history over the phone to screen out those women whom we cannot accept. We make certain a prospective patient is in her early pregnancy and, through our questions, decide if she seems to be in good physical health. When she comes for her first visit, we will examine her very carefully to be reasonably certain she will have a normal pregnancy. Husbands are invited to come along.

FIRST PRENATAL VISIT: This is the most important visit, and we usually spend up to an hour with each new patient. We explain our program in detail and give her the opportunity to find out everything she wants to know, from hospital rules, to the way we practice, to the hospital fee. We explain that she will meet a different midwife at each visit so that she will know us all by the time she is ready to deliver.

At this first visit, we take a complete medical and obstetric history; then the patient is given a thorough physical examination, including a pelvic. Blood and urine are taken along with a Pap smear and a cervical smear for laboratory examination.

At the end of the visit, the patient is given another appointment four weeks later, along with our answering-service number. If she has any problems that cannot wait until her next visit, we want her to feel free to call us. We are available 24 hours a day. She receives a schedule of the parent-education classes given in the hospital (though she is free to attend classes anywhere she chooses) and a list of pediatricians, one of whom she must choose to examine her baby before discharge from the hospital. She also receives a prescription for the vitamins and iron she will need during her pregnancy.

SUBSEQUENT PRENATAL VISITS: At the second visit, four weeks later, the patient is again examined, though not internally this time, and given the complete results of the laboratory findings. We are careful never to keep any facts hidden and are pleased to have her look over her charts if she wishes. If we find that she has medical problems that may possibly preclude a normal birth, we tell her that she must be in the care of an obstetrician. Again, we answer all questions.

Thereafter, the patient comes in for an examination every four weeks until approximately the twentieth week. At this point, we ask her to come every week until we can hear the fetal heartbeat. In the twenty-eighth week, any patient with a family history of diabetes is given a glucose tolerance test to evaluate the blood sugar level. If it is abnormal, she must be transferred out to a physician.

In the second trimester (fourth to sixth month) of the pregnancy, the patient comes to our offices for examination every two to three weeks, and toward the end of the pregnancy, every week.

Pelvic examinations are not performed again until the last three weeks of pregnancy when we want to find out if there are any changes in the cervix—dilatation (opening) or effacement (thinning)—which might indicate an imminent labor and delivery.

Toward the end of the nine months, we discuss (along with anything else the patient wants to talk about) the prepared-childbirth methods and techniques and go over the signs of labor. She is told to let us know immediately if her membranes rupture and to call us as soon as she notices regular contractions or any other unusual sign.

EARLY LABOR: We like to keep our patients at home as long as possible in early labor if we know she is safe and comfortable. There is no reason for a woman to spend this time in the hospital; it is better for her to be home and going about her normal business at this time.

On the other hand, she must keep us constantly informed of her progress, and we insist she check in with us by telephone every few hours. If there is any uncertainty about her condition, we ask her to come to the hospital for examination.

FIRST STAGE OF LABOR: When the patient is in active labor, she comes to the hospital. The midwife accompanies her to the labor room, and she will remain there throughout labor and delivery. The patient is introduced to the obstetric nurse, usually the only other person she will see during labor, who will come in periodically to check her blood pressure, fetal heartbeat, etc.

The midwife makes an initial physical examination to determine how much the cervix has dilated, how much it has thinned, the position of the baby, and the station of the baby's head.

The father coaches the patient (with our help, if necessary) with her breathing and relaxation techniques and provides most of the early support and encouragement if he can. The midwife is there to help him, explain what is going on with the labor, interpret the findings of the fetal monitor if one is used, and generally provide company and support as well as make certain everything is proceeding normally. If it is requested, she gives medication.

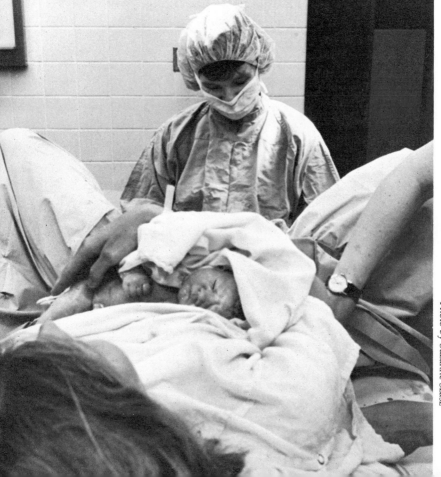

Photo by Suzanne Szasz

As I have explained, if there are any questions of complications, the midwife consults with the back-up obstetrician.

Toward the end of the first stage, as the contractions become stronger, the patient—who is encouraged to labor in any position she finds most comfortable—usually wants little conversation and more guidance.

TRANSITION: When the cervix is dilated 7 or 8 cm. and the baby's head is well down in the pelvis, the midwife works with the couple more and more, explaining what is going on, assisting the patient with her breathing, and helping her to remain in complete control of her contractions.

SECOND STAGE: As the baby descends in the birth canal, the patient, if she is having her first baby, is encouraged to push until the fetal head can be seen during a contraction. The father supports one leg and the midwife the other during the pushing. Each push must be carefully controlled by the midwife so that the perineum begins to stretch slowly. If the patient has had previous babies, she does not usually push in the labor room.

THE DELIVERY: When the baby is ready to deliver, the patient is moved in her bed to the delivery room and transferred to the table. At this point, everything must be well coordinated, and the patient is asked to listen to only one voice—the midwife's. The nurse monitors the fetal heartbeat, the nurse-anesthetist sits at the head of the table on the off chance that she/he may be needed, the father supports the patient's shoulders. Her legs rest in stirrups, which are dropped very low and close for maximum comfort, and two pillows or a birth wedge raise her into a semisitting position.

The patient is then told when and how much to push so that the head advances slowly and gently and is encouraged to watch the baby's progress in the overhead mirror. If an episiotomy is needed to prevent tearing, it is done at this time.

The baby's head is delivered smoothly, and the baby begins to cry as its face is wiped and the mucus is removed from its mouth. Then the shoulders are delivered, and the rest of the baby follows.

When the cord stops pulsating, it is clamped, and the baby is wrapped in a sterile blanket and given to the mother to hold and breast-feed.

THIRD STAGE: In a few minutes, the placenta or afterbirth is then delivered and examined. If there has been an episiotomy, it is now repaired with stitches, using a local anesthetic.

POSTNATAL: After birth, the newborn is taken to the nursery until the temperature has stabilized, then to the mother's room, where he/she will stay until they are discharged from the hospital. The mother, accompanied by the father, goes directly to her room. Because she has not been drugged, she has no need of the recovery room.

The pediatrician will examine the newborn and report his findings to the parents.

The midwives, along with the nurses and the infant-care technicians, supervise mother and baby during their two-day stay in the hospital.

On the morning of the third day, the patient and her baby are discharged unless, for some reason, she wishes or needs to stay longer.

While mothers must from this point on call their pediatrician if they have questions about their baby, they are encouraged to call us if they have any problems themselves. We are always available to them as long as they need us.

Four weeks after the delivery, we see the patient again to examine her and make certain everything is returning to normal, to discuss and provide family planning, and to inquire about the newborn's well-being.

Photo by Suzanne Szasz

Nurse-Midwifery Services
in the U.S.

The following is a list of nurse-midwifery services in the U.S. at this writing. Most are clinics or military hospitals, but a growing number will take private patients.

Because the list changes constantly, I suggest, if you are interested in a midwifery service near you, that you write or call the American College of Nurse-Midwives, 1000 Vermont Avenue, N.W., Washington, D.C. 20005. Telephone: 202-628-4642.

ALABAMA
Hospital
Maxwell Air Force Base
Montgomery, Alabama 36112

ALASKA
USPHS Alaska Medical Center
Box 7-741
Anchorage, Alaska 99501

ARIZONA

Hospital
Davis-Monthan Air Force Base
Tucson, Arizona 85707

Maricopa County Hospital
2601 E. Roosevelt
Phoenix, Arizona 85006

Memorial Hospital
1201 South 7th Avenue
Phoenix, Arizona 85007

USPHS Indian Hospital
P.O. Box 649
Fort Defiance, Arizona 86504

CALIFORNIA

Los Angeles County—University of Southern California Medical Center
Women's Hospital
Los Angeles, California 90033

Martin Luther King Jr. General Hospital
Los Angeles, California 90059

St. Luke's Hospital
San Francisco, California 94110

Watts Health Foundation
Los Angeles, California 90059

CONNECTICUT

Drs. Borelli, Foye, McGrade, and DeGrazia
Route 7 Professional Building
Brookfield, Connecticut 06804

Community Health Care Plan
150 Sargent Drive
New Haven, Connecticut 06511

Drs. Friedman, Molumphy, and Olson
860 Howard Avenue
New Haven, Connecticut 06510

Hill Health Center
428 Columbus Avenue
New Haven, Connecticut 06519

Yale Health Plan
17 Hillhouse Avenue
New Haven, Connecticut 06511

Yale–New Haven Hospital
789 Howard Avenue
New Haven, Connecticut 06510

Yale University School of Nursing
Graduate Program in Maternal and Newborn Nursing
   and Nurse-Midwifery
38 South Street
New Haven, Connecticut 06510

DISTRICT OF COLUMBIA

D.C. Department of Human Resources
1875 Connecticut Avenue, N.W.
Washington, D.C. 20009

D.C. General Hospital
19th Street and Massachusetts Avenue, S.E.
Washington, D.C. 20003

Georgetown University School of Nursing
Nurse-Midwifery Program
Washington, D.C. 20007

Group Health Association
2121 Pennsylvania Avenue, N.W.
Washington, D.C. 20037

FLORIDA

Bethesda Memorial Hospital
Boynton Beach, Florida 33435

R. B. Cuthbert, Jr., M.D., F.A.C.P.
Mortan F. Plant Hospital
323 Jeffords Street
Clearwater, Florida 33516

Hospital
Elgin Air Force Base
Valparaiso, Florida 32542

Hospital
MacDill Air Force Base
Tampa, Florida 33608

Laurent Radkin, M.D., and Denise Juba, C.N.M.
Live Oak, Florida 32060

University Hospital
655 West 8th Street
Jacksonville, Florida 32209

GEORGIA

Archibald Memorial Hospital
with Thomas County
Thomasville, Georgia 31792

Dr. T. Schley Gatewood
Americus, Georgia 31709

Glynn-Brunswick Memorial Hospital
Brunswick, Georgia 31520

Grady Memorial Hospital
80 Butler Street, S.W.
Atlanta, Georgia 30303

GUAM

Naval Regional Medical Center

Seventh Day Adventist Clinic—affiliated with Guam Memorial Hospital

ILLINOIS

Chicago Board of Health and Illinois Masonic Medical Center
Coordinated Nurse-Midwifery Service
834 West Wellington
Chicago, Illinois 60657

Health and Hospitals Governing Commission of Cook County
Cook County Hospital
1835 West Harrison Street
Chicago, Illinois 60612

The University of Illinois at the Medical Center
College of Nursing, Department of Maternal-Child Nursing
Nurse-Midwifery Program
P.O. Box 6998
Chicago, Illinois 60680

KENTUCKY

Appalachian Regional Hospital
Hazard, Kentucky 41701

D. G. Barker, M.D.
Hindman, Kentucky (Knott County) 41822

Buckhorn Clinic *
Perry County, Kentucky

---

* Write to sponsor:
National Health Service Corps
U.S. Department of Health Education and Welfare
Health Services and Mental Health Administration
Rockville, Maryland 20852

Frontier Nursing Service
Wendover, Kentucky 41775

Ireland Army Hospital
Fort Knox, Kentucky 41775

Lake Cumberland District Health Department
Somerset, Kentucky 42501

Lend-a-Hand Center
Walker, Kentucky (Knox County) 40997

J. Myron Lord, M.D.
Frankfort, Kentucky 40601

Morehead Clinic
Morehead, Kentucky 40351

University of Kentucky Medical Center
Lexington, Kentucky 40506

MAINE

Maine Medical Center
22 Bramhall Street
Portland, Maine 04102

MARYLAND

Baltimore City Hospital
Baltimore, Maryland 21224

Johns Hopkins Hospital
Department of Obstetrics and Gynecology
600 North Broadway
Baltimore, Maryland 21205

Johns Hopkins University
School of Hygiene and Public Health
Department of Maternal and Child Health
Baltimore, Maryland 21205

Mercy Hospital
Department of Obstetrics and Gynecology
301 St. Paul Place
Baltimore, Maryland 21202

Peninsula General Hospital
Department of Obstetrics and Gynecology
Salisbury, Maryland 21801

Provident Hospital
Department of Obstetrics and Gynecology
2600 Liberty Heights Avenue
Baltimore, Maryland 21215

United States Air Force
Nurse-Midwifery Program
Malcolm Grow USAF Medical Center
Andrews Air Force Base, Maryland 20031

MICHIGAN

Women's Hospital
1045 East Ann Street
Ann Arbor, Michigan 48104

MINNESOTA

Hennepin County General Hospital
Department of Obstetrics and Gynecology
5th and Portland
Minneapolis, Minnesota 55415

University of Minnesota Hospital
Department of Obstetrics and Gynecology
Powell Hall
Minneapolis, Minnesota 55414

MISSISSIPPI

Delta Community Hospital and Health Center
Mound Bayou, Mississippi 38762

Mississippi State Board of Health
Bureau of Family Health Services
P.O. Box 1700
Jackson, Mississippi 39205

South Washington County Hospital
Hollandale, Mississippi 38748

University of Mississippi Medical Center
2500 North State Street
Jackson, Mississippi 39216

MISSOURI

St. Louis Department of Health and Hospitals
1515 Lafayette
St. Louis, Missouri 63104

St. Louis University School of Nursing & Allied Health
Professions
1401 South Grand Boulevard
St. Louis, Missouri 63104

NEBRASKA

Ehrling Berquist Hospital
Offitt Air Force Base
Omaha, Nebraska 68113

NEVADA

Hospital
Nellis Air Force Base
Las Vegas, Nevada 89101

NEW HAMPSHIRE

Wentworth Douglas Hospital *
Dover, New Hampshire 03820

* Nurse-Midwives are employed by:
Strafford County MIC Program
791 Central Ave.
Dover, New Hampshire 03820

NEW JERSEY

Atlantic City Medical Center
1925 Pacific Avenue
Atlantic City, New Jersey 08401

Jersey City Medical Center
(previously Margaret Hague Maternity Hospital)
Clifton Place
Jersey City, New Jersey 07304

New Jersey Medical School
Martland Hospital
Department of Obstetrics and Gynecology
Division of Midwifery
65 Bergen Street
Newark, New Jersey 07101

North Hudson Hospital
Weehawken, New Jersey 07087

NEW MEXICO

Hospital
Kirtland Air Force Base
Albuquerque, New Mexico 87110

Indian Health Service Hospital
Shiprock, New Mexico 87420

NEW YORK

Albany Medical Center, Department of Obstetrics, Albany, New York 12208

Beth-Israel Medical Center, 10 N.D. Perlman Place, New York, New York 10003

Brookdale Hospital Center, Linden Boulevard and Rockaway Parkway, Brooklyn, New York 11202

Brooklyn-Cumberland Medical Center, 39 Auburn Place, Brooklyn, New York 11205

Brooklyn Jewish Hospital, 667 Eastern Parkway, Brooklyn, New York 11213

Childbearing Center, 50 East 92nd Street, New York, New York 10028

Columbia-Presbyterian Medical Center, Sloane Hospital for Women, 168th Street and Broadway, New York, New York 10032

Downstate Medical Center, State University of New York, 450 Clarkson Avenue, Brooklyn, New York 11226

Elmhurst Hospital, Queens, New York 11373

Flower-Fifth Avenue Hospital, 5th Avenue and 106th Street, New York, New York 10029

Gouverneur Hospital, 9 Gouverneur Slip, New York, New York 10002

Harlem Hospital Center, Lenox Avenue and 135th Street, New York, New York 10037

Jacobi Hospital, Pelham Parkway and Eastchester Road, Bronx, New York 10461

King's County Hospital, 451 Clarkson Avenue, Brooklyn, New York 11203

Lenox Hill Hospital, New York, New York 10021

Lincoln Hospital, Concord Avenue and 141st Street, Bronx, New York 10454

Mount Sinai Medical Center, 5th Avenue and 100th Street, New York, New York 10029

Maternity, Infant Care—Family Planning Projects, New York City Department of Health, 377 Broadway, Suite 718, New York, New York 10013

New York Hospital, 525 East 68th Street, New York, New York 10021

Roosevelt Hospital, 428 West 59th Street, New York, New York 10019

St. Luke's Hospital, New York, New York 10025

St. Mary's Hospital, 1298 St. Mark's Avenue, Brooklyn, New York 11213

University of Rochester Medical Center, Rochester, New York 14627

OHIO

Cincinnati General Hospital
Cincinnati, Ohio 45229

Cleveland Metropolitan Hospital
Cleveland, Ohio 44109

Hospital
Wright Patterson Air Force Base
Fairborn, Ohio 45433

Our Lady of Mercy Hospital, Mariemont
Cincinnati, Ohio 45227

St. Ann's Hospital
Columbus, Ohio 43205

St. Luke's Hospital
Cleveland, Ohio 44104

Simpson Center for Maternal Health
350 South Burnett Road
Springfield, Ohio 45505

OREGON

Dr. Donald F. Woomer
750 Eleventh Avenue, East
Eugene, Oregon 97401

PENNSYLVANIA

Booth Maternity Center
6051 Overbrook Avenue
Philadelphia, Pennsylvania 19131

McKeesport Hospital
1500 Fifth Avenue
McKeesport, Pennsylvania 15132

Temple University Hospital
Department of Obstetrics and Gynecology
3401 North Broad
Philadelphia, Pennsylvania 19140

PUERTO RICO

Puerto Rico Department of Health
1306 Ponce de Leon Avenue
Santurce, Puerto Rico 00908

School of Nurse-Midwifery
University Hospitals
Caparra Terrace
Puerto Rico 00922

SOUTH CAROLINA

Nurse-Midwifery Program
Medical University of South Carolina
80 Barre Street
Charleston, South Carolina 29401

Marjory Wells, C.N.M., S. L. Collins, M.D., and A. J.
   Villani, M.D., P.A.
1501 Ninth Avenue
Conway, South Carolina 29526

SOUTH DAKOTA

Public Health Service Hospital
Pine Ridge, South Dakota 57770

TENNESSEE

Halston Valley Community Hospital
Kingsport, Tennessee 37662

Nurse-Midwifery Program
Department of Nursing Education
Meharry Medical College
Nashville, Tennessee 37208

Nurse-Midwifery Service
Maternal and Infant Care Project
Woodlawn Extended
Dyersburg, Tennessee 38024

TEXAS

Bexar County Hospital District
(Robert B. Green Hospital)
527 North Leona
San Antonio, Texas 78207

Hospital
Sheppard Air Force Base
Wichita Falls, Texas 76306

Su Clinica Familiar
152 South 6th Street
Raymondville, Texas 78580

UTAH

Family Practice Clinic, Holy Cross Hospital
1045 East 1st Street
Salt Lake City, Utah 84103

Hospital
Hill Air Force Base
Ogden, Utah 84406

Uintah County Hospital
Vernal, Utah 84078

University of Utah
College of Nursing
25 South Medical Drive
Salt Lake City, Utah 84112

Utah State Department of Health
45 Fort Douglas Boulevard
Salt Lake City, Utah 84112

VERMONT

Associates in Obstetrics and Gynecology
40 Colchester Avenue
Burlington, Vermont 05401

University of Vermont
College of Medicine
Department of Obstetrics and Gynecology
Given Medical Building
Burlington, Vermont 05401

VIRGIN ISLANDS

Charles Harwood Memorial Hospital
Christian sted, St. Croix, U.S. Virgin Islands 00802

Knud-Hausen Memorial Hospital
Charlotte Amalie, St. Thomas, U.S. Virgin Islands
00801

VIRGINIA

Hospital
Langley Air Force Base
Virginia 23365

St. Mary's Hospital
910 Virginia Avenue
Norton, Virginia 24273

WEST VIRGINIA

A. Ray Jacobson, M.D.
P.O. Box 50
Beckley, West Virginia 25801

Your Own Childbirth Record

For a permanent record of your pregnancy and delivery, fill in the blanks in the chart below. You will appreciate having the facts later.

Date of last menstrual period:

Baby's estimated birth date:

First appointment:

Second appointment:

    Laboratory findings:

    Blood group:

    Pap smear:

    Other:

    Blood pressure:

    Weight:

    Subsequent appointments:

    Fetal heartbeat (date first heard):

Comments:

Onset of labor (date and hour):

Rupture of membranes:

Admission to hospital:

First stage of labor:

Transition:

Delivery:

Method of Delivery:

Baby's Apgar score:

Weight:

Length:

Method of feeding:

Circumcision:

Discharge from hospital:

Pediatric follow-up appointment:

Postpartum checkup:

Family Planning:

Comments:

Selected Readings

ARTICLES

Ander, Nina. "Return of the Midwife." *Good Housekeeping.* September 1975.

Browne, H. E., and Isaacs, G. "The Frontier Nursing Service: The Primary Care Nurse in Community Hospital." *Am. J. Obstet. Gynecol.* 124:14. January 1976.

Burnett, J. E. "A Physician-Sponsored Community Nurse-Midwife Program." *Am. J. Obstet. Gynecol.* 40:719. November 1972.

Comer, Nancy Axelrad. "Midwifery: Would You Let This Woman Deliver Your Child?" *Mademoiselle.* June 1973, p. 134.

Gatewood, T. S., and Stewart, R. B. "Obstetricians and Nurse-Midwives: The Team Approach in Private Practice." *Am. J. Obstet. Gynecol.* 123:35. September 1975.

Harris, D.; Daily, E. F.; and Lang, D. M. "Nurse-Midwifery in New York City." *Am. J. Public Health* 61:64. January 1971.

Hogan, A. "A Tribute to the Pioneers." *Journal of Nurse-Midwifery* 20:6. Summer 1975.

Klaus, Marshall H., M.D., et al. "Human Maternal Behavior at the First Contact with Her Young." *Pediatrics* 46:187–192.

———. "Maternal Attachment: Importance of the First Post-Partum Days." *New England J. of Med.* 286:460–463.

Lake, Alice. "Childbirth in America." *McCalls.* January 1976, p. 83.

Levy, B. S.; Wilkinson, F. S.; and Marine, W. M. "Reducing Neonatal Mortality Rate with Nurse-Midwives." *Amer. J. Obstet. Gynecol.* 109:50. January 1971.

Lubic, Ruth W. "Myths about Nurse-Midwifery." *Amer. J. of Nursing* 4:268–9.

———. "The Midwife in the United States: Report of a Macy Conference." Josiah Macy Jr. Foundation, 1968.

Maech, J. S. "Obstetrician-Midwife Partnership in Obstetric Care." *Am. J. Obstet. Gynecol.* 37:314. February 1971.

Montgomery, T. A. "A Case for Nurse-Midwives." *Am. J. Obstet. Gynecol.* 105:309. October 1969.

Morrone Wardell, Wenda. "Which Way Do You (and He) Want to Have Your Baby." *Glamour.* May 1976, p. 164.

Record, J. D., and Cohen, H. R. "The Introduction of Midwifery in a Prepaid Group Practice." *Am. J. Public Health* 62:354. March 1972.

Slome, C.; Wetherbee, H.; Doly, M.; Christensen, K.; Meglen, M.; and Thiede, H. "Effectiveness of Certified Nurse-Midwives." *Am. J. Obstet. Gynecol.* 124:177. January 1976.

Steinmann, Marion. "Now the Nurse-Midwife." *The New York Times Magazine.* November 23, 1975, p. 34.

Stern, C. A. "After Office Hours, Midwives, Male-Midwife and Nurse-Midwives." *Am. J. Obstet. Gynecol.* 39:308. February 1972.

BOOKS

Arm, Suzanne. *Immaculate Deception.* Boston: San Francisco Book Company/Houghton Mifflin Books, 1975.

Bean, Constance A. *Methods of Childbirth.* New York: Doubleday, 1972.

Better Homes and Gardens Baby Book. New York: Bantam Books, 1972.

Bing, Elizabeth. *Six Practical Lessons for an Easier Childbirth.* New York: Bantam Books, 1969.

———. *Moving Through Pregnancy.* New York: Bantam Books, 1975.

The Boston Women's Health Book Collective. *Our Bodies Ourselves.* New ed. New York: Simon & Schuster, 1976.

Bradley, Robert A. *Husband-Coached Childbirth.* New York: Harper & Row, 1974.

Brazelton, T. Berry. *Infants and Mothers: Differences in Development.* New York: Dell Publishing Co., 1969.

Buryn, Ed; Brown, Janet; Lesser, Eugene; and Mines, Stephanie. *Two Births*. New York: Random House Bookworks, 1972.

Caplan, Frank. *The First Twelve Months of Life*. New York: Grosset & Dunlap, 1973.

Chabon, Dr. Irwin. *Awake and Aware: Participating in Childbirth Through Psychoprophylaxis*. New York: Delacorte, 1966.

Cherry, Sheldon H. *Understanding Pregnancy and Childbirth*. New York: Bobbs Merrill, 1973.

Chess, Stella; Thomas, Alexander; and Birch, Herbert G. *Your Child Is a Person*. New York: Simon & Schuster, 1965.

Cohen, Allen, and Walzer, Stephen. *Childbirth Is Ecstasy*. San Francisco: Aquarius Publishing Co., 1971.

Colman, Arthur and Libby. *Pregnancy: The Psychological Experience*. New York: The Seabury Press, 1973.

Davis, Adelle. *Let's Have Healthy Children*. New York: Harcourt, Brace & World, 1951.

Dick-Read, Dr. Grantly. *Childbirth Without Fear*. New York: Harper & Row, 1970.

Eden, Alvin, N., and Heilman, Joan Rattner. *Growing Up Thin*. New York: McKay, 1975.

Eiger, Marvin S., and Olds, Sally Wendkos. *The Complete Book of Breastfeeding*. New York: Bantam Books, 1972.

Ehrenreich, B., and English, D. *Witches, Midwives and Nurses*. New York: The Feminist Press, 1973.

Ewy, Donna and Roger. *Preparation for Childbirth*. Colorado: Pruett Publishing, 1970.

Flanagan, Geraldine Lux. *The First Nine Months of Life*. New York: Simon and Schuster, 1962.

Forman, Alice M.; Fishman, Susan H.; Woodville, Lucille, eds. *New Horizons in Midwifery*. Proceedings of the Sixteenth Triennial Congress of International Confederation of Midwives, October 28–November 3, 1972. Washington, D.C. Published 1973, Waverly Press, Baltimore.

Fraiberg, Selma H. *The Magic Years*. New York: Charles Scribner's Sons, 1959.

Guttmacher, Alan F. *Pregnancy and Birth*. New York: Signet, 1962.
———. *Pregnancy, Birth and Family Planning*. New York: Signet, 1973.

Hall, Robert E. *Nine Months' Reading*. Rev. ed. New York: Bantam Books, 1973.

Hazell, Lester D. *Commonsense Childbirth: How to Have Your Baby Your Way*. New York: G. P. Putnam's Sons, 1969.

Hellman, L. M., and Pritchard, Jack A. *Williams Obstetrics*. 14th Ed. New York: Appleton-Century Crofts, 1971.

Homan, William E. *Child Sense*. New York: Bantam Books, 1970.

Karmel, Majorie. *Thank You Dr. Lamaze: A Mother's Experience in Painless Childbirth*. Philadelphia: J. B. Lippincott, 1959.

Kitzinger, Sheila. *Giving Birth: The Parents' Emotions in Childbirth*. New York: Taplinger Publishing Co., 1971.

———. *The Experience of Childbirth*. New York: Taplinger Publishing Co., 1972.

La Leche League International. *The Womanly Art of Breastfeeding*. Franklin Park, Illinois: La Leche League, 1963.

Lamaze, Fernand. *Painless Childbirth: The Lamaze Method*. New York: Pocket Books, 1972.

Leboyer, Frederick. *Birth Without Violence*. Paris: Seuil, 1974.

Marzallo, Jean. *9 Months, 1 Day, 1 Year*. New York: Harper & Row, 1975.

Maternity Center Association. *A Baby Is Born*. New York: Grosset & Dunlap, 1964.

———. *Guide for Expectant Parents*. New York: Grosset & Dunlap, 1971.

McBride, Angela Barron. *The Growth and Development of Mothers*. New York: Harper & Row, 1973.

Milinaire, Caterine. *Birth*. New York: Harmony Books, 1974.

New Moon Communications. *Proceedings of the First International Childbirth Conference*. Stamford, Connecticut: New Moon Communications, 1973.

Pomeranz, Virginia, and Schultz, Dodi. *The First Five Years*. New York: Doubleday, 1973.

———. *The Mothers' Medical Encyclopedia*. New York: New American Library, 1972.

Pryor, Karen. *Nursing Your Baby*. New York: Pocket Books, 1972.

Salk, Lee. *Preparing for Parenthood*. New York: Bantam Books, 1975.

Spock, Dr. Benjamin. *Baby and Childcare*. New York: Pocket Books, 1968.

———. *Raising Children in a Difficult Time*. New York: W. W. Norton & Co., 1974.

Spotnitz, Dr. Hyman, and Freeman, Lucy. *How To Be Happy Though Pregnant*. New York: Berkley Publishing Co., 1974.

Vellay, Pierre. *Childbirth Without Pain*. Translated by Denise Lloyd. New York: E. P. Dutton & Co., 1959.

Index

About the Authors

Barbara Brennan, C.N.M., is the chief nurse-midwife at Roosevelt Hospital in New York City. She received her nurse-midwifery education at Kings County Hospital in Brooklyn, and has delivered more than 2,000 happy, healthy babies.

Joan Rattner Heilman is a writer and mother of three children. Her most recent book was *Growing Up Thin*, with Dr. Alvin Eden.